Paul Mi

CW01426132

Sebastian

To Make IT
on
TIME

Translation: Paul Mikulicz
Proofreading: Karolina Kadluczka
Techical Correction: Karolina Kadluczka
Cover and graphic design: Malgorzata Sokolowska, InkWander
Text Compostion: InkWander

ISBN: 9788397063068

Limitless Mind Publishing Ltd
15 Carleton Road
Chichester
PO19 3NX
England
Tel. +44 7747761146
Email: office@limitlessmindpublishing.com

Dear Reader!

Find us on Facebook/Instagram:
limitless mind publishing

And visit our page on Amazon
by entering: limitless mind publishing into the search bar
or by scanning the QR code to see our other titles.

♥ *We would greatly appreciate your opinion. It means a lot to us.*

For my son

From the author

Whatever you can do or dream you can, begin it! Boldness has genius, power, and magic in it.

Johann Wolfgang von Goethe

Imagine the moment when your life is turned upside down. That feeling when you suddenly have to face another illness that strikes your child without warning. This story will take you on a journey into the unknown, leading from loud heavy metal concerts to church prayers. It's a tale of unwavering determination by parents who confront another painful challenge. After three years of relative peace, their lives are shuffled once again. The whirlwind of emotions, love, stress, and helplessness returns with double force.

You'll discover that maintaining composure is the key to keeping emotions in check. You'll learn how to act to do what's best for your child. You'll uncover the deepest corners of your heart. "To make it on time" is not just the story of one family but also an inspiring reminder of the strength we possess when we love and fight for our loved ones.

So, let's start from the beginning...

Table of Content

Introduction

Love is the humblest yet the most powerful force that the human being has.

Mahatma Gandhi

This is already my second book that was not supposed to exist at all! And yet... Life unfolded in such a way that I wrote another story straight from the heart. But before I begin, let's go back six years, when our son, Sebastian, was born.

It was December 2015. My wife and I were eagerly awaiting the birth of our first child. For Christmas, my mom came over with my younger brother. We spent a peaceful Christmas Eve, and shortly after, the delivery was to take place.

The weather outside was not kind. Instead of snow, it was raining, and at times, a stronger wind blew. We all wondered what our little son would look like. How much hair would he have on his head? What color would his eyes be?

I kept my hand on my wife's belly, eagerly awaiting the birth of our child. On the scheduled delivery day, we went to the hospital. Upon arrival, we approached the reception desk. The lady at the window pointed us in the direction of the maternity ward. I rang the bell, placing my finger on the intercom. They let us in. At the registration, I mentioned that my wife's due date was today. While waiting for a response, I set down a pink bag on the floor that we had brought from home. It was quite heavy. We had no idea what to pack, so we stuffed everything we thought might come in handy into the bag.

The young brunette sitting across from me told us to go back home if there were no contractions yet. We were in shock. We didn't expect the procedures to be like this. So, we went back home and explained to my mom what they had told us at the hospital. It was already late, so we went to bed.

While in deep sleep, I was awakened by the light in the bedroom being turned on. Eve said she wanted to go to the hospital right away because contractions had started. I washed my face with cold water to wake up, got dressed, and then helped my wife down the stairs and put on her jacket. We headed towards the car. The bag was already in the trunk. We hadn't had a chance to take it out since our previous visit.

Once at the hospital, we went straight to the delivery room. Eve wanted to give birth to Sebastian in a pool. Unfortunately, for a water birth, labor needed to be shorter. So, they moved my wife to a bed. There, she received gas anesthesia, and after more than the longest twenty hours of our lives, she gave birth. Eve, holding our son for the first time, burst into tears, but they were tears of happiness. We did it! On December 30th, our son, Sebastian, came into the world. I was deeply moved. An incredible feeling overwhelmed me. I had never been so happy before. Routine checks were performed on the little one. Then, when everything was fine, we were discharged to go home.

It was winter. We dressed the baby in warm clothes, gently placed him in the car seat, covered him with a blanket, and headed for the exit.

Initially, parenthood seemed very challenging to us. We slowly learned how to take care of a small child. All the dry theories we had heard before turned out to be insufficient. Reality was completely different, and to make matters worse, my wife experienced postpartum shock. Fortunately, after some time, this state passed for her. We were enjoying life. We watched our child grow, take their first steps, and utter their first words.

When Sebastian was a little over three years old, our daughter was born. We wanted to give him a sibling. Unfortunately, the prenatal diagnosis revealed that the girl would be born with a spina bifida in the lumbosacral region. And so it happened. Subsequent complications led to our daughter fighting for her life for over six months from the moment of birth. The spina bifida itself was not as serious as the complications that arose over time. The daily struggle for Natalie's health, trips to the hospital, stress, tears, hospice, emotions, helplessness, and the battle with doctors - all of this was with us almost every day. However, I won't go into detail right now because you can read her entire story in my first book, "Natalie: Only Faith Remains."

Our life went on. There were better days and worse ones. The children were growing. I worked at a warehouse, and my wife took care of the home. Everything changed in February 2022, a few days after my thirty-second birthday. Unfortunately, life once again presented us with a challenging ordeal. We had to face another nightmare that returned after more than three years.

Shock and Disbelief

Never deprive anyone of hope; it might be all they have.

H. Jackson Brown Jr.

It was Thursday, the third of February, the day of my thirty-second birthday. I had taken the day off from work to spend it with my beloved family.

Snowflakes were falling outside the window. I gazed through the window at the gently falling snowflakes while savoring a freshly brewed cup of coffee. After a while, the rest of the household woke up and offered heartfelt birthday wishes. I cherished every moment.

We dressed Sebastian for school. After breakfast, I dropped him off for his lessons. On my way back, I stopped by the store for some small errands. I always looked for a checkout with a cashier at the supermarket. I found the self-checkout machines incredibly annoying as they often malfunctioned.

I returned home, unpacked the groceries, and sat in the living room with a cup of green tea. My daughter came to me for a hug. I took her out of her walker and placed her on the couch next to me. She cuddled up to me, resting her little head on my stomach. Snow was still gently falling outside, and we were savoring the moment.

After a while, I picked her up and we went to play in her room. Playing with her favorite shopping basket, Natalie played the role of the shopkeeper, and I was the customer. There was a toy kitchen nearby that we would start playing with right after finishing our shopping

game. Our daughter loved preparing various dishes with plastic vegetables and fruits.

As for Eve, she drove to the store to get the birthday cake, which I
had forgotten to buy. I wasn't a big fan of cakes, but a delicious apple
pie was always a welcome treat at home. I stashed the purchased slice
of cake in the fridge. We wanted to wait until Sebastian returned from
school. In the meantime, I received a few phone calls with well-wishes
from family members. After playing with our daughter, we went downstairs. Natalie sat at the kitchen table in a specially adapted chair, and
she began drawing on a large sheet of paper. Meanwhile, I put on some
water for our favorite coffee, which both Eve and I were in the mood
for at that moment. I sat in the kitchen across from our daughter, waiting for the kettle to whistle. In between calls, I glanced at social media from time to time.

I had to blow out the candles with the numbers three and two at
around 4:30 PM. It was already dark outside, with the only light coming from the streetlamp. Snow continued to fall, and we spent the
evening as a family, playing various board games and watching our
favorite movies.

The next morning, I had to get up for work. We put the kids to bed
around 8 PM. After such a wonderfully spent day, I went to bed. I was
tired. I set the alarm for four in the morning and fell asleep in an instant.

When I returned home the next day, Eve told me that Sebastian had
a slight cough. She added that he had gone to school as usual. I reassured her that it wasn't anything serious. His body would likely fight it
off, and if home remedies didn't help, we could see a doctor for antibiotics to ease the child's discomfort.

Before picking up our son from school, I went to the gym. This
year, I had obstacle course races planned, so I was focusing on my fitness. After finishing the training, I headed straight to the school. I picked up Sebastian at 3:30 PM. Indeed, he coughed lightly from time to
time. The winter season always brought various illnesses into our
home, mostly just colds.

Back at home, we gave him raspberry compote. Sebastian drank two cups of the warm beverage. He was very tired, so he went to sleep. Eve and I reviewed his school notes. He had to work on writing letters and numbers, and there was also a small book for him to read. We both agreed that the homework could wait until Sebastian felt better. We had time as all the assignments were due the following week.

Our son woke up in the evening. He didn't get out of bed; he just shouted for Mom to bring him some compote upstairs. Eve wasn't sure whether to send him to school the next day. While putting Natalie to bed, I told Eve to message me at work the next day. I wanted to know if the child went to school or stayed home.

We went downstairs to watch TV for a bit. Eve came to check on Sebastian from time to time, measuring his temperature. We went to bed around 10:30 PM.

Upon waking up in the morning, I peeked into our son's room. He was sweating profusely and sleeping restlessly, tossing and turning while uncovering himself. I woke up Eve and told her to call and make an appointment at the clinic at 7 AM when the reception would open. I knew the weather conditions weren't favorable for going out, especially with a small child in a stroller. However, I had to take the car in the morning to get to work. I also told her to make sure to let me know what the doctor said and what medication he prescribed.

During my break at work, which started at 10:30 AM, I checked my phone. I hadn't received any updates from my wife yet. There was nothing, just some notifications, emails, and other less important things. Another ten minutes passed when I received a message from Eve. The doctor had determined that Sebastian had a clear chest. He advised the child to drink plenty of fluids and rest at home. No antibiotics or other medication were prescribed. If the child developed a fever, he should be given children's paracetamol to lower it. This message reassured me.

After my break, I returned to the warehouse. My shift ended at 2 PM. After work, I went straight to the gym for my training. My main challenge for this year was the Ultra Warrior race - five hours of running, with a route filled with obstacles, mud, and fire. Each lap of the course was about twelve kilometers long. The goal was to complete as many laps as possible within a set time limit. My race was scheduled for June, so I had plenty of time to prepare. The Spartan Race World Championships in Greece, which were supposed to take place in November, were still uncertain due to the pandemic. Nobody knew if they would postpone the event to the following year, as they had done in the previous two years. It was a total gamble. The organizers assured that this year, restrictions would be eased, and the event would take place.

After finishing my workout, I returned home. Sebastian was resting, playing video games while covered with a blanket. Next to him on the living room table, there was a cup of warm compote. I asked my wife how our son was feeling. She replied that he still had a cough like the day before but was drinking more fluids to fight off the cold. I spent the rest of the day with him. We played racing video games together to lift his spirits. He had been quite interested in fast cars for some time. He had already gathered quite a collection of toy cars he played with daily, mostly with me. Sebastian didn't like to play alone, and he always needed company. On that day, all the sports cars remained untouched. He didn't feel like playing with any toys. He went to bed quite early. It wasn't even nine o'clock, and Sebastian was already in bed, hugging his favorite plush toy. For some unknown reason, he always fell asleep in a fetal position. He curled up into a ball and instantly fell asleep. Tired from the whole day, we also went to bed, putting Natalie to sleep first.

I woke up for work feeling sleep-deprived. I kept waking up during the night and heard Eve going to our son's room to check on him. Fortunately, he had slept through the night, but he woke up all sweaty in the morning. His clothes were as wet as if someone had poured a bucket of water on him.

I went to work. Before getting into the car, I asked Eve to keep me updated on whether our son's condition was improving or worsening. I couldn't focus on my tasks, constantly thinking about what was happening at home, especially since Natalie also required care and rehabilitation. I wanted to be at home, but my financial situation didn't allow for it.

By the end of my shift, I received only one update that Sebastian was still sweating but didn't have a fever. I returned home after 2 PM. The child was playing video games again. It was clear he was getting bored, and the fast cars helped him pass the time. Indeed, he was sweating all the time, and his clothes had to be changed three times that day.

My wife told me that the next morning she would call the clinic again. She would ask them to reexamine him and prescribe some antibiotics so that he wouldn't suffer. She did just that, but the doctor, after the examination, determined that there was nothing wrong with the child. His chest was clear, and he recommended continuing with plenty of fluids, explaining that colds were quite common during the winter.

Another day passed. In addition to the cough, a fever appeared. Sebastian was sweating continuously, whether he was covered or not. Once we managed to lower the temperature, it returned after about two hours. We gave him a children's medication so that he could sleep through the night. These situations left me quite exhausted. Early mornings for work and helping at home drained the last of my energy. Due to exhaustion, I increased my caffeine intake. I had to give up my training for those few days. Assisting at home was now the top priority.

Time passed, but the cold didn't let up. The temperature kept rising and falling. It was a cycle of fever, then a break, followed by its return.

To make matters worse, our child started to look pale. He showed significant signs of fatigue. He lost his appetite for everything, even his favorite food didn't taste good to him.

While at work, I received a call from my wife. She asked me to leave work for the day and come home. She wanted to take him to the emergency room for an examination.

I rushed home immediately after work. I left the car engine running in the driveway. Eve, along with Sebastian and Natalie, was already waiting at the door. We put the kids in the car. I made sure the house was locked, then we hit the road.

I focused on driving, making my way to the hospital. It was a thirty-minute drive. In the meantime, the hospital ward had been informed that we were on our way and would arrive in twenty minutes. We reached the hospital.

Eve went to the emergency room with Sebastian, and I stayed in the car with Natalie. It was cold, so we didn't want to take her out of the car. While waiting for updates, the car windows began to fog up. From time to time, I started the engine while parked to warm it up.

Shortly before noon, I received a call, and Eve told me they needed to perform a few more tests. They would likely stay in the hospital overnight. Sebastian still had a fever. We decided that I would go back home and pack the most essential items. He needed plenty of extra clothes at the moment.

I returned home with Natalie. I changed her clothes, played her favorite cartoon, and began packing a bag. As I was folding my son's favorite shirt and putting it in the bag, the phone rang. I could only hear crying on the other end of the phone, which was something I was already very familiar with. I didn't want to, but I firmly told her to tell me what was going on. From experience, I knew that this was the only way I could calm her down.

A long moment passed, and she finally managed to say something. Specifically, after a blood test, it turned out that our child had an extremely low level of platelets. An immediate transfusion at the children's hospital in Leeds was necessary. She added that they were preparing an ambulance to transport her and Sebastian. Then she burst into tears even more and could barely say that they suspected leukemia.

I asked, "What kind of leukemia?" I asked her to tell me everything more clearly. I couldn't piece together the chaotic information she was giving me. She only managed to calm down a little. The doctors, seeing the symptoms, had tentatively mentioned that it might be leukemia, but detailed examinations would be carried out in Leeds.

I was stunned. The first thought that came to my mind was that the doctors were scaring us again. How many times had that happened when we were fighting for Natalie's life? Constant fear and a focus on the worst possible outcomes. The pattern was all too familiar to me. I asked Eve to calm down, knowing it probably wouldn't help. I knew my wife too well, but I had no other choice but to offer those words. Just before ending the call, I let her know that I would come to the hospital tomorrow by train with Natalie, and we would sort everything out calmly. I hung up.

In my mind, an image appeared automatically from over three years ago. Those flashes. The platform, the train, the journey to the hospital, the homeless man with a long gray beard sitting with his dog near a tree near the entrance, the shop, the bright corridor, and that sign... "Welcome to the Children's Hospital" hanging on the bricks just before the main entrance. I shook myself out of my thoughts, and shivers ran down my spine. I hadn't expected the situation to take this turn. As someone who had spent a lot of time in the hospital with their second child, I knew that not everything checked out after the initial diagnosis.

On that day, I didn't call Eve again. I just asked her to rest whenever she found the time. Evening arrived. I put Natalie to bed and continued packing bags. In total, I had a backpack and one large pink bag. I placed all the necessary items for changing my daughter into her small backpack. Everything was prepared for our trip the next day.

In the meantime, I checked online for my train schedule. With my mind full of thoughts, I went to sleep. I knew that the following day would be long and challenging.

Welcome back, Mr. Paul

If we were meant to stay in one place, we'd have roots instead of feet.

Rachel Wolchin

The alarm clock rang at six in the morning. As is often the case in the winter, it was still dark outside. Fortunately, it wasn't raining. The weather forecast indicated clear skies and sunshine for today, but a cold day ahead. The temperature was around one degree Celsius.

Natalie was still asleep. I went downstairs to prepare breakfast. Scrambled eggs with bacon should give us the energy we need for the journey. When I turned off the stove, the child woke up with a gentle cry because there was no one upstairs. I hugged her and brought her downstairs still in her pajamas. While going down the stairs, I whispered in her ear that we would get her dressed after breakfast to avoid getting her clothes dirty.

The time to leave home was approaching. We had twenty-five minutes until the train, and the station was a fifteen-minute walk away. I always tried to leave with some extra time to comfortably reach our destination. While putting on her tiny shoes, I realized that a diaper change was necessary. These things happen, I thought. We would just have to walk a bit faster to catch the train. I slung a pink bag over my shoulder and a gray backpack. I tied Natalie's small beige backpack to the stroller.

I didn't want to take the car. The parking fee at the hospital was astronomically high. Besides, I still remembered how difficult it was to drive in Leeds when we went for the same hospital for Natalie's ultra-sound with Eve. Somehow, I had only a minute left when I ran onto the platform. Due to lack of time, I couldn't buy tickets from the machine.

I calmly sat in the carriage and waited for the conductor to come. I used to do this sometimes. In England, it was always possible to buy tickets from the conductor without any issues. But not that day. Unfortunately, on this route, there was a ticket inspection, and the lady, who looked like a stickler for her job, insisted that I should receive a fine. The railway regulations clearly state that passengers must have purchased tickets before boarding the train. I explained my situation and the urgency of being at the hospital. I added that tickets could always be purchased from the conductor. The stubborn and unpleasant lady didn't listen. She didn't give a damn about my situation.

Issuing a £20 fine, you could see a smile on her face. The only response she gave me was that I could describe the situation I told her by filing an application to cancel the fine online. I hated people like her who found joy in harming others. So, I accepted that unfortunate piece of paper. I had neither the time nor the desire to argue with some dumb lady. I had a little child in a stroller, two backpacks, and a bag. What would have happened if she had asked me to get off and wait for the police? I just moved on.

Thirty minutes into the journey passed. The train stopped at the Leeds destination station. As I got off the train, I could once again observe the rat race: men in suits with briefcases looking at their watches, ladies in heels fixing their makeup in a small mirror, people in constant rush. The pursuit of money was very visible there in general.

I stood in a small queue to exit. At the stroller gate, I showed the fine instead of tickets. But now, the fine wasn't my concern. I wanted to get to the hospital as quickly as possible. The road to the facility we used to visit three years ago, almost every day for five months, came back to me as if it were yesterday. However, this time it was different. Previously, we made this journey with Sebastian, and today it was with Natalie. The street noise and endless construction works once again reminded me that I wouldn't want to live in a big city. Living in Poland from birth until my twenty-first year, that's how it was. A large, beautiful, but horribly noisy city – Gdynia, my hometown. The dimensions of my hometown could be compared to Leeds.

Returning to reality, we approached the bridge over the road, just before the hospital. As we descended from it, on the left, there was a torn tent by a tree. An elderly man with a long gray beard was staying there. I remembered him well. I used to pass him every time my daughter was in the same hospital. Passing by the tent, you could see a pile of garbage and a sleeping dog. I passed him. During this time, my daughter said, "Daddy, look, a dog!" I turned to the right and saw the previously mentioned sign on a white background: "Welcome to the Children's Hospital." It should have said, "Welcome again, Mr. Paul..."

Entering the building, masks were still mandatory, which I didn't like. However, the situation didn't allow me to figure out how not to wear them here. On the main corridor, I turned right, as that was the ward where my son was transferred with my wife.

Approaching the intercom, I took a deep breath. I tried to reduce my stress as much as I could. I pressed the gray button, around which a green LED was lit. A lady from the reception answered, asking about the purpose of my visit. She let me in. I walked to the reception, which was on the right. Before I could say anything to the receptionist, the phone rang. The young woman asked me to wait for a moment because she had to answer it. However, it turned out to be a longer moment. It lasted almost five minutes. When the white handset was put down, the brunette turned her gaze toward me. She smiled and asked how she could help.

After explaining the situation, she directed me to a specific room. However, we couldn't enter with Natalie. Hospital pandemic procedures stipulated that only one adult could be with the child, and children were not allowed to enter. So, I called Eve and asked her to come to the reception. After a moment, she appeared near the reception. Natalie smiled when she saw her. It was evident from my wife that she was deeply affected by the situation, but she didn't return the smile. She only took Natalie to the waiting room just before the ward entrance. I told her I would stay with our son for a while and join them shortly. I skipped saying "don't worry" this time. It wouldn't have the desired effect I was hoping for. I knew it from experience a few years ago.

I entered the room. Before I checked on my son, I saw the familiar machines constantly monitoring the patient's condition. Some families had their places cordoned off by curtains, while others didn't. After a moment, I pulled aside the curtain behind which my son's bed was located. He looked at me but didn't say anything. After a while, he turned his gaze toward the television. I sat next to him and offered my hand. He grabbed it and squeezed it tightly. A familiar cartoon was playing on the TV. When I was Sebastian's age, my friends and I used to watch it regularly. I remember that when it was broadcast on a now-defunct TV channel, the neighborhood would empty out. Sebastian continued to hold my hand very tightly. He was too tired to say anything. There were IV lines attached to his tiny hand. The blood had been transfused overnight. Now, various medications were flowing through the cables, the names of which I didn't know.

We watched the animated series for about ten minutes. I told him I had to go to Mom for a moment and would be right back. Sebastian didn't want to let go of my hand. He desperately wanted me to stay with him.

I gently loosened his fingers, explaining that I would return shortly. He responded with a sad look, barely asking me to come back quickly. I looked at my son, keeping my hand on the curtain. Sebastian was just changing the TV channel. Tears streamed down my cheeks.

Once again, I found myself in a place where I never wanted to be. After more than three years of peace, everything came back like a boomerang. However, I had a faint hope that this time we would leave this cursed place quickly. I pulled the curtain closed behind me.

Heading towards the reception, I encountered a nurse on the way. She was on duty with Sebastian that day. I asked her to call me or Eve if our son became restless. I also mentioned that we were in the waiting room just behind the doors.

The doors were closed, so I knocked and said it was me. Eve opened the door, and Natalie smiled, shouting, "Daddy!"

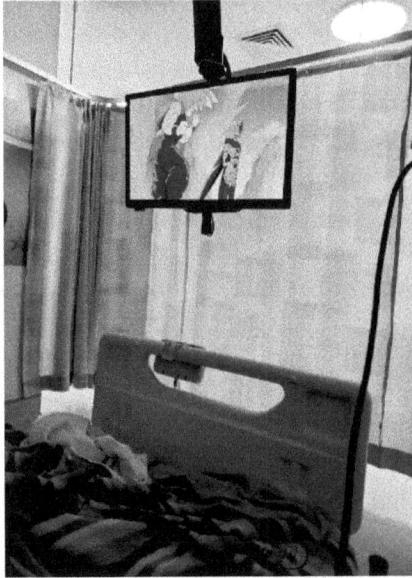

My first visit to my son in the hospital

I asked Eve to tell me everything from the moment she arrived at Wakefield Hospital up until today. With tears in her eyes, she told me everything. An urgent blood transfusion had to happen as soon as possible. Doctors at Wakefield Hospital suspect leukemia, but detailed tests are scheduled in the coming days.

I comforted Eve, telling her not to cry until we have the test results. Now, I wanted to spend some time with our son. I was trying to be strong, but it was all just a facade. Taking Sebastian's hand once again, I broke down in tears, kneeling by his bedside. I kept saying to myself, "My son... First Natalie, and now Sebastian in the hospital." I began to blame God for everything. I wanted Him to give us some peace at last! I started asking myself, "Why us again?" The child didn't seem to notice that I was crying. He must have been on strong medications, which I hadn't had a chance to ask the staff about. It seemed like the emotions had to come out one way or another. I wiped my tears with a paper towel.

After a while, the doctor came into the room. I sat in a chair and focused on the information he wanted to share. I listened to everything, learning about the current medications and the doctors' suspicions. I thanked him. The doctor glanced at the patient card hanging by the bed and then left the room. While the nurse adjusted my son's medications, I held my head in my hands. I couldn't gather my thoughts. I said goodbye to my son, promising to come back to him tomorrow.

I returned to my girls. Due to the winter season, I didn't want to take the child back home at night. I said goodbye, hugging my wife. As I left the facility, I looked at the building. It was already dark outside. I sighed and made my way to the platform, leaving behind shoeprints in the snow. On the platform, I stood in line at the ticket counter. After purchasing my ticket, I went to a small cafe nearby. I ordered my favorite cappuccino with chocolate. It was cold, even on the platform, so the warm drink helped me warm up.

Sipping on a hot beverage, I boarded the train and headed back home. I put Natalie to sleep, then turned on the computer in her room. Amidst all the chaos, I had forgotten to mention the morning ticket I received. I took the crumpled ticket out of my wallet, laid it on the desk in front of me, and started searching online for information on how to appeal the ticket. I went to the railway website and found the form. I described the entire situation and sent the message. I turned off the computer, went downstairs to the living room, and started streaming a TV series online.

I woke up in the middle of the night. The TV was still on. I couldn't remember when I had fallen asleep on the couch. I looked at the clock, and it read 3 o'clock in the morning. I went upstairs, set the alarm for 6 AM.

To my surprise, I woke up in the morning before the alarm went off. Natalie was still asleep. Just like the day before, I went downstairs to prepare breakfast. Today, it was an omelet with raspberry jam. Unfortunately, I could only give the child a small amount of food. The rest had to go through the gastrostomy. We ordered special food for Natalie from the pharmacy.

After breakfast, we headed to the platform on time. This time, I managed to buy the tickets from the machine on the platform. I hesitated before buying the monthly ticket. I didn't know how long Sebastian and Eve would stay in the hospital.

The weather took a turn for the worse that day. A chilly wind started to blow, and instead of snowflakes, raindrops fell from the sky. The temperature was above freezing. The snow that had fallen a few days ago had already melted. I checked the departure board. It turned out that my train was delayed, and a few minutes later, it was completely canceled!

There was another railway station ten minutes away. From that platform, I could also get to Leeds, but the only difference was the train. It had only two carriages instead of four and was older and less comfortable. I just wondered if I could use the tickets I had purchased on it. I didn't have much time. I headed to the other station and made it onto the train three minutes before the scheduled departure.

As if the conductor had something to object to, I took a photo of the schedule at the South Elmsall platform. I wanted to have proof that my train had been canceled. My concerns were dispelled by the railway employee in a light blue uniform. He clearly stated that I could use this ticket in such a situation. When I got off in Leeds, I made my way to the dull gray building as usual.

Sebastian was asleep. I took my wife's place in the room. Eve went to attend to Natalie, and I stayed with our son. Even though he was asleep, I wanted to be by his side. The child's condition remained unchanged. When he woke up, he simply grabbed my hand and squeezed it tightly. He kept staring at the TV the whole time. His lips were slightly swollen, most likely a side effect of some of the medications.

Suddenly, the doctor entered from behind the curtain and asked if I was the child's father. I replied that I am. He introduced himself by name and specialty. He also mentioned that he would be scheduling a consultation with me and my wife in the coming days. He added that a bone marrow biopsy would be necessary for testing. This procedure was meant to verify whether our son had leukemia or not. Written consent was required for the child to undergo general anesthesia. When the doctor moved on to other patients, I promised my son that I would buy

The information board about the delayed train in South Elmsall, which was completely canceled a few minutes later.

him a set of building blocks to play with tomorrow. There were toys in the hospital, but he didn't seem interested in playing with any of them. Those weren't the wisest words, though. Only afterward did I realize that I would receive my paycheck next Friday. The account wasn't looking good. But as they say, a promise is a promise.

I said goodbye to my son and returned to Eve. Time flew by quickly in the hospital, and as the sun set, I made my way back home.

Diagnosis

You gain strength, courage and confidence by every experience in which you really stop to look fear in the face. You are able to say to yourself, 'I have lived through this horror. I can take the next thing that comes along.' You must do the thing you think you cannot do.

Eleanor Roosevelt

The next day, as I was getting ready to leave, the phone rang. It was Eve calling. She informed me that the consultation had been scheduled for Thursday, February tenth. It was exactly a week after my birthday. It was supposed to take place at noon so that I could comfortably reach the hospital. She also added that today they would take the child for a bone marrow test. From her voice, it was clear how stressed she was about the upcoming examination, not to mention the result.

My journey to the facility went unchanged. Today, however, I stopped by the store to pick up the promised set of building blocks. Sebastian's favorite universe was Star Wars, so I was looking for the cheapest set. I managed to find a small set for eighteen pounds. The box contained a small construction and two figurines. I couldn't wait to give the present to my son. I didn't expect to see a smile on his face, considering he was on such strong medications. For Natalie, I bought a separate figurine, and she was delighted, smiling in my direction. The package was tightly packed. Natalie didn't want any help and tried to open it herself all the way to the hospital.

We arrived. Natalie and I waited for Eve in the room near the ward. When she came, Natalie was delighted once again, showing her mom the gift from dad. I went to Sebastian. I handed him the gift, looking at him with a smile. Unfortunately, my smile was forced. Beneath the mask, there was sadness, helplessness, and powerlessness. Sebastian thanked me for the gift, but he couldn't smile due to his swollen lips. He only asked me to assemble it for him. Without hesitation, I opened the box and spread the contents on the portable table from which Sebastian ate his meals. The assembly didn't even take me twenty minutes. The child began to play with the figurines, then fell asleep holding them in his hands.

I went to the kitchen to make some coffee and grab a snack. There was a small kitchen on the ward with a fridge, a few cabinets, and a microwave. Then I went to the waiting room to discuss the upcoming consultation with my wife. Together, we decided that I would come earlier due to the unpredictable train schedule. It wasn't yet known at what time they would take the child for the examination. It was already getting dark, so I returned home and waited for further information.

I read the message only in the morning. I was very tired from my daily commutes. I read that everything had gone according to plan, and we had to wait for the results. Today was the day. Thursday, the tenth of February. A very serious conversation with the doctor awaited us. I had no choice but to embark on my monotonous journey. I wanted to get there as quickly as possible and get this ugly consultation over with. I tried to think positively. My subconscious told me that the bone marrow results would show nothing serious. After all, doctors make mistakes too.

I arrived at the place. Before the conversation, I spent some time with my son. We watched cartoons, played with building blocks. I kept checking the clock every ten minutes. The closer it got to noon, the more I began to sweat and worry. You can't cheat time. Finally, the long-awaited hour arrived. The doctor in glasses and the man in a purple outfit from the foundation entered the room. We all sat down, and they offered us coffee or tea. I took white coffee with milk, and my wife declined. The conversation proceeded calmly. The person in the room had over a decade of experience in their profession. He made us aware that we had to wait for the test results. He added that all the symptoms indicated leukemia. I thought to myself that it was probably just more talk and scare tactics. I tried to think positively, but something would hold me back from time to time.

In the back of my mind, I had images from over two years ago. I didn't want to find myself in such an awful situation again at any cost. The conversation continued. They even established a preliminary treatment plan without having the test results yet! Suddenly, the doctor's phone received a message. Fate had it that everything they said turned out to be true. Our child had Acute Lymphoblastic Leukemia. I didn't know what to say. Being experienced in conversations with doctors, I asked directly: Is it curable? I had to react quickly. I didn't want my wife to burst into tears. In response, we heard that it was curable, but the treatment lasts three years for boys and two years for girls. It was a completely different consultation from a few years ago when Natalie was given no chance of survival. I was convinced that this strong argument would allow me to talk calmly with my Eve. Thankfully, I asked about it.

Turning my gaze away from the doctor, I looked at Eve, who appeared calm. She wasn't crying. She focused only on the facts. Apparently, she realized that crying wouldn't change anything, and we needed to focus on treatment to get rid of this mess as soon as possible. The person leading the meeting was surprised that none of us shed tears. He asked where our composure came from. I replied that we had already had contact with this hospital. I added that the little girl sitting in the pushchair almost died here, and we have experience in dealing with such situations.

Flipping through another A4 sheet of documentation, we learned how it would all look. First and foremost, the child cannot be discharged home. No one can tell us how long he'll stay in the hospital. We also learned that for the first six months, Sebastian will have intensive treatment. Doctors asked us not to leave the country or go on any vacations during this period. They didn't want to overwhelm us with too much information at once. We wouldn't be able to remember it all. We focused on the upcoming weeks. It's hard to determine how long that consultation lasted that day.

I absorbed all of this information, but the most important thing was that the disease is curable. It just requires a long period of treatment. When the meeting ended, I spent a few more minutes with Eve to discuss a few matters. One thing was certain. I needed to buy a monthly train ticket. Secondly, we decided that I would take care of Natalie, and Eve would stay in the hospital with Sebastian. I would commute every day and help as much as I could. At that moment, we couldn't come up with anything else.

I returned to the room to say goodbye to my child and tell him that I would be back tomorrow. On the train ride back, I sat my daughter next to me. I stared out the train window, organizing my thoughts. I couldn't believe that this was happening again. I so desperately wanted to believe that it was a bad dream and not real. Why us again? Why can't this hospital leave us in peace? These were questions without answers. I knew I couldn't give in and let my emotions take over. I vividly remembered how much stress and nerves it had cost me to fight for Natalie's life. Yes, my psyche had become more resilient, but apparently not enough to face this new threat.

The next day, I called my clinic and requested a conversation with my doctor. I had an appointment at 9 a.m. I intentionally scheduled it early because my entire day was already planned out. When I was in the doctor's office, I explained the situation and asked for a two-month leave from work. Then I drove to work and informed them about the dire situation I was in. The next step was the trip to Leeds and buying a monthly ticket for the following day. Once I was in the city, I waited in line at the ticket counter for about five minutes. The woman behind the glass handed me the ticket and showed me the price. I reluctantly placed my credit card on the terminal. The price was very high, but I had no other choice. On that day, I had to pay over a hundred pounds for a piece of plastic! Compared to the amount from two years ago, it was more expensive. Much more expensive. Money was disappearing from my account at an alarming rate. Being in a big city every day was draining my finances at every turn. There were still a few days left until payday. I had to figure out a way to manage.

I only had coffee when I was in the small kitchen for parents on the ward. The rest of the day was no different from the previous ones. I fell into a routine. Leaving the house with my daughter to catch the train, going to the hospital, talking to my wife, spending time with my son, back on the train, back home, putting the child to sleep, the alarm clock in the morning, and so on. I had to prepare myself for the fact that my next few months would look exactly like this.

The Worst Day of My Life

Patience and perseverance have a magical effect before which difficulties disappear and obstacles vanish.

John Quincy Adams

Rain was pouring and a strong wind was blowing outside. On this day, I was supposed to bring clean clothes for Sebastian and my wife from home and take the old ones back with me. I packed two backpacks and a small bag.

Taking a deep breath, I opened the front door of our house. I dressed the child warmly, and I covered the stroller with a rain cover. As we headed to the platform, I held the stroller's handle with one hand and the rain cover with the other to keep it from flying away in the wind. Despite being securely attached, it would lift up from the leg side when the wind blew harder.

Walking against the wind, I reached the platform. Of course, I wasn't surprised that the train was delayed once again. Initially, the announcement said the delay would only be ten minutes. It ended up being over thirty minutes late. Fortunately, there was shelter at the train station - a small one with three red seats and a ticket vending machine standing nearby. It provided us with some refuge from the nasty weather.

As we headed towards the hospital, I had to keep holding the rain cover with one hand to prevent it from flying away. I didn't want my child to get cold. I was so relieved when we arrived. It was warm inside. I immediately took off my jacket and Natalie's. My pants were completely soaked, including one sock.

On the way, I stopped on a damaged sidewalk slab that wobbled a bit. All the water from the slab ran straight into my shoe. When I saw my wife, I handed her the backpacks and the bag. The dirty clothes were prepared in three plastic bags, which were placed on the floor next to the dresser. I was planning to pack them just before leaving the hospital. However, I preferred to do it now so I wouldn't forget later. I had gathered quite a bit of them. The backpack was stuffed, and the zipper barely closed.

Even though I hadn't left the hospital yet, I suspected that in such weather and with so many bags, the journey back wouldn't be easy. But I didn't go there to complain. While spending time with my son, I noticed that his lips were still swollen. The child had his mouth open all the time. My wife said they would provide some remedies or ointment to reduce the swelling. I was also informed that the first round of chemotherapy would be administered to the child in two days. The doctors needed to perform additional tests to ensure they could safely administer the medication.

In the kitchen, apart from free coffee, there were various kinds of snacks like energy bars and chips. It wasn't healthy, but I didn't have any other food with me, so I indulged in these products.

Every few days, I brought pre-made meals from the supermarket for my family. Sebastian didn't always want to eat what they served him in the hospital. He loved spaghetti the most. The medical staff made it clear that the child had to eat if he didn't want a nasal feeding tube. You could see a few children on the ward with a small white tube inserted into their nostrils.

On that day, I wanted to stay an extra hour longer than usual. The weather wasn't improving, and I knew the return home would be exhausting. I played with my son with a set of blocks I had recently bought for him. He loved Star Wars, especially the villains.

From time to time, when Sebastian wanted to go to the bathroom, I held the IV pole from which medications were flowing. My son walked very slowly. He was weak, very weak, even after a blood transfusion. Every time, I watched his steps carefully. They looked as if the child was about to fall. It was definitely not a sight I wanted to see. I had to find a way to cope with it. Sometimes, I wanted to hold his hand, but he refused, saying that he could manage on his own.

It was getting late. I said a gentle goodbye to my son, hugging him carefully. I didn't want to damage any of the cables connected to his IV lines. Together with Natalie, we said goodbye to Mom. We headed towards the exit. I tied one backpack to the handlebar. The other was on my back, and I had a bag slung over my shoulder with a wide strap. Laden with bags, I exited the facility, pushing the stroller. When the automatic exit doors opened, I felt a huge gust of wind and rain. Next to the exit, a few people were standing in slippers and bathrobes, smoking their cigarettes. Some of them even had IVs that they had to hold firmly to prevent nature from sweeping them away.

I was very hungry, so I went to a familiar American chain for a pancake with crispy chicken. My child fell asleep in the stroller. I had enough time to eat my meal leisurely. I still had thirty minutes until the train, and the place I was in was five minutes away from the station. At the station, surprisingly, there were many travelers for that hour. Most of them were looking at the information board with slight confusion.

In my small favorite café, I was tempted to have some coffee to warm up a bit. I went to my platform, 9B, where my train was departing. The information showed a 20-minute delay. I waited, but the train didn't arrive. Thankfully, the child didn't wake up. When I looked at all the platforms around, it turned out that everyone was waiting for their delayed trains. I quickly checked in the app to see what could be the reason. It turned out that due to sudden rainfall and bad weather conditions, the tracks were flooded, and all trains were suspended until further notice!

I couldn't believe it. I was left without a return train with a small child in a stroller, two backpacks, and a bag full of clothes. I called my wife and asked if there was a possibility to return to the hospital and spend the night. Unfortunately, there was no such possibility. The hospital staff cited regulations and the conditions of the ongoing pandemic. I had to come up with something.

A taxi would have cost me around fifty pounds for the ride. While it would have gotten me home, I had already spent money on a monthly ticket. I opted for the cheaper but more exhausting option. From Leeds to Wakefield, I took bus number 110. Then, from Wakefield to South Elmsall, I took bus number 496. It was the same company, so I could use the same day ticket. I headed to the respective bus stop, and what happened? The bus was canceled! I felt defeated. My child woke up hungry and started crying. There was a small shop nearby, but at this hour, almost everything was sold out. I grabbed some snacks from the shelf and wondered if another bus would arrive, scheduled in twenty minutes. My child's hunger was temporarily satisfied, but I continued to wait, checking the departure board. The bus finally arrived. I bought a ticket from the driver and glanced at my watch from time to time. I had less than five minutes to make the transfer at Wakefield bus station. I prayed to make it on time. It was the last bus going towards my destination! If I missed it, I would have to take a taxi, incurring additional substantial costs.

The rain was pouring relentlessly. The bus driver was driving very slowly, adding to my stress. He stopped at almost every bus stop since bus stops in England are on-demand. Passengers were boarding and disembarking constantly. Time was running out, and I didn't know if I'd make it. The final stretch, just one more intersection, and I'd be at the bus station. Of course, at the last moment, the traffic light turned red. I could see my second mode of transportation at the station. I arrived with less than a minute to spare. I got off the bus, quickly approaching with all my bags in hand. The bus was already pulling away. I began frantically waving to the driver, pointing at the child in the stroller. He stopped. He opened the doors and let us on. I thanked the elderly gentleman behind the wheel of the bus. I could finally breathe a sigh of relief. There was another forty minutes of travel ahead. Given the weather conditions, the journey could take longer. Natalie fell asleep halfway.

I arrived in my town. Getting off the bus, I thanked the driver once again. The rain continued, and the wind had intensified. I had to walk on foot from the bus stop to my doorstep, which took less than ten minutes. I had to keep stopping to adjust the rain cover. I finally made it home. Upon arriving, I took off my wet shoes and clothes. I was soaked through and exhausted.

After putting my daughter to bed, I sat on the couch. My thoughts wandered far away. I took a moment to rest. I got up to turn on the computer. First, I sent a message to Eve on my phone, letting her know we had arrived home. Then, I checked my email. There was an unread message from the railway company. I opened it and started reading. It turned out that my appeal had been rejected! The message clearly stated that it was my fault. I was given a deadline of seven days to pay the fine. I had no strength left to appeal again. I paid the fine later that same day. I was on the brink of a breakdown.

I closed my eyes, leaned my head back, and began to think more intensely about the hopeless situation my family was in. This time, it was hitting me harder. Suddenly, a few drawers in my mind unlocked. I decided to do something to help my son in any way I could. I would post publicly on my social media about the situation my family was facing. Despite the late hour, I wrote a post. I also decided to start a fundraising campaign. We were practically out of money, and we had two sick children. I didn't know what to do in such a hopeless situation.

I sat at the computer until late into the night. I started reading various pieces of information on how to organize such a fundraising campaign. I jotted down the most crucial details on a piece of paper and went to sleep. The next day, I wanted to discuss my idea with Eve and find out what she thought about it.

Milestone

Courage is resistance to fear, mastery of fear, not absence of fear.

Mark Twain

The weather had improved. It was no longer raining, but the sky remained overcast. The forecast indicated that there should be no rain today. I checked on an app if the trains were running today. I tried to find information on the internet about whether they had fixed the track in Leeds, but to no avail. Every article was just a description of how this situation had paralyzed rail traffic. I was hopeful that they had fixed the issue. I also considered that it might not have been that simple, and rail traffic could still be suspended.

I didn't set an alarm that day. I decided that I needed to recover from yesterday's exhausting journey. I didn't call Eve either. I just sent a message saying that I would come today, but I didn't know what time. It all depended on whether the trains would be running. I didn't feel like taking the buses or driving through the city center. Eternal traffic jams and roadworks always made it difficult to get to the hospital.

I dressed Natalie, put her in the stroller, and left the house. I arrived at the train station. I glanced at the departure board. It turned out that the malfunction had been fixed. To my surprise, the train arrived on time. We boarded the carriage, and the train set off on its journey. I left the stroller a bit further away. I took Natalie and sat her next to me. She was happy to watch the views through the window. However, I was lost in thought. Since morning, a very strange feeling accompanied me, one that I couldn't describe. I really don't know what happened to me, but

I felt calm. Just yesterday, my hands could tremble from stress, but today, nothing. Perhaps it was also due to it being payday? I don't know.

Before heading to the hospital, I stopped by a store to buy a few ready-made meals for Sebastian and my wife. I didn't have time to cook at home; all I had were breakfasts and dinners. Lunch was out of the question. I picked up two lasagnas and two portions of spaghetti. I also got some drinks and snacks. When I arrived, I handed everything to Eve so she could label the meals to make sure no one took them from the fridge by mistake. I heard such situations had happened before. I spent some time with Sebastian. I took his first picture, which I intended to post on my social media. I explained my plan to my wife, what I was specifically aiming to do. She was skeptical, but she agreed. This way, I could help.

I decided that if I didn't try, I would never know if it was worth it. I discussed my idea only with Eve. I didn't want to seek opinions from others because they could be divided. I had to find out for myself if it made any sense. Meanwhile, while we were talking, the doctor came to us to discuss a few things. We were presented with a list of products that Sebastian should not consume under any circumstances. The list included all yogurts, kefir, bottled water, pickles, liquid egg yolk, and so on. Everything that contained natural bacterial flora. If our son consumed these products during chemotherapy, it wouldn't be effective. We were told that it would significantly interfere with the drugs Sebastian had to take.

The next part of the conversation was about how Sebastian would receive chemotherapy. There were two options. The first was hanging tubes, and the second was a tiny port under the skin. The doctor advised us to agree to these tubes because they would be attached permanently during three years of treatment. However, if we opted for option number two, they would have to insert a needle into the port every time, then administer the drug, and remove the needle. We had two days to make the decision before the first chemotherapy session. New information was coming in, and we had to somehow organize it in our heads.

It was quite essential to write everything down in a notebook. There was too much data to remember it all. That day, I didn't want to take risks as I did the day before. I left the facility at the same time as usual to ensure I had plenty of time to catch my return train. I allowed myself enough time to have lunch on the way back. The return train arrived on time.

Being back home, I only had to put the child to sleep, sit at the computer, and get to work. I looked at the monitor. I had no idea how to write the description. I wanted to put this into words so that people could understand the seriousness of the situation. Through trial and error, I managed to set up a fundraiser on my social media. Sebastian enjoyed extreme sports with me, so the photo attached to the fundraiser was taken at one of the sports events. The treatment was going to last for three years, so I set the target at £5,000. I stared at the "Publish" button for over five minutes. At that moment, anxiety consumed me. I was sure I had to try something new to help my son to the best of my ability.

It happened. With a single mouse click, I posted the message on my profile, pinning it at the top of my timeline. It read:

"Little SPARTAN needs your help!! Hello everyone! In February 2022, our son was unexpectedly diagnosed with ACUTE LYMPHO-BLASTIC LEUKEMIA, which is a type of aggressive cancer that turned our lives upside down! The treatment is planned for the next 3 years and will require a 50 km (30 miles) journey to the hospital and back at least 4 times a month. Then, after 3 years of chemotherapy, our son faces another 5 YEARS of disease recurrence checks! Sebastian requires a special diet and, later on, immune system-supporting supplements. If you can, please share this post on your timeline, and we will be very grateful for your help."

I asked my mom and a friend if they could help me check the fundraiser. I wanted to transfer a few bucks just to see if everything was working as it should. My mom's transfer came through immediately. However, for some unknown reason, my friend couldn't make the payment, and some error kept popping up.

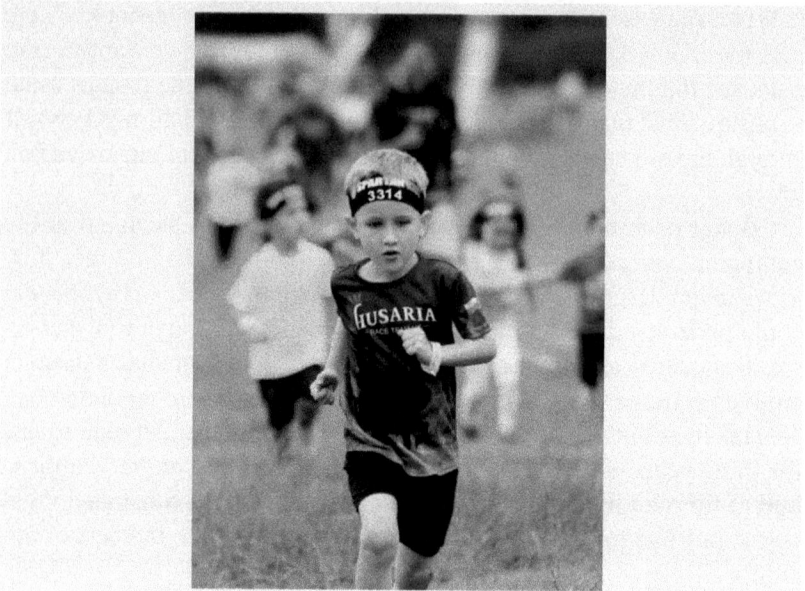

The photo of Sebastian that I attached to the fundraising post.

It was getting late, so I told him I had to go to bed and asked him to let me know if it worked later and what the cause of the error was. I shut down the computer, gave Natalie a goodnight kiss on her cheek, and then went to bed. I silenced my phone. I decided I would check how my post was received only in the morning.

In the morning, when it was already light, I went downstairs to make myself a brewed coffee with a little xylitol. Only after I sat at the kitchen table, I decided to check my phone. I had so many notifications and private messages that I didn't know where to start. First, I looked at the fundraiser. To my surprise, it had been shared more than ten times already, and the first donations had started to appear. Then, I looked at the private messages and started reading. Some people expressed their sympathy and wished a speedy recovery. Others mentioned they had trouble making a donation to the fundraiser and asked for the bank account number. I was really positively surprised by the response! To be honest, I was afraid my post would be ridiculed, but it turned out to be the opposite! I kept wondering why some people could donate without any issues while others encountered an error? I began replying to everyone, both in private messages and comments.

It was time to catch the train. As I headed towards the train station, the sun was shining. The temperature was around one degree Celsius. I dressed Natalie warmly so she wouldn't catch a cold. While sitting on the train, I thought about what had happened. In fact, almost every person who shared my fundraiser added their comment, asking others to share it further. It was truly incredible. How many people with kind hearts got involved in our cause! When I reached the Leeds platform, I went to a shop to grab another coffee. I was terribly sleep-deprived, and I still had to reach the hospital. While sipping a delicious cappuccino, I wanted to check the comments on the fundraiser. Unfortunately, I received a message that I had run out of phone credit. I wanted to top up my phone, but to do so, my phone stubbornly needed an internet connection. Oh well, I put it back in my pocket and waited to connect to the free hospital Wi-Fi.

Once at the hospital, Eve asked me why I didn't let her know at what time I would be arriving. I explained that I had run out of credit, so I couldn't top up my phone. I showed her the fundraiser and the description and photo I had provided. Surprisingly, it had already been shared more than thirty times. New comments were popping up as well. Eve was astonished that my idea had taken off. She had expected that nobody would be interested in our situation. We talked for a while. Then, I went to the room where the little warrior was lying. I had prepared a small surprise for him. I printed three sheets with some very important things and characters for him. Despite his lack of enthusiasm for everything, he was delighted. I took scissors and tape from my backpack and attached all the sheets above his bed. Sebastian asked me if I could change the TV show to a different cartoon. When I did that, he held my hand gently and asked if I could stay and watch cartoons with him. I told him I would love to watch cartoons together. Spending time with my son was bringing us closer. Perhaps I wanted to make up for the time we had spent saving Natalie's life? I didn't have an answer to that question. Nonetheless, there had to be something to it, even though more than three years had passed since the previous events. We watched a cartoon together.

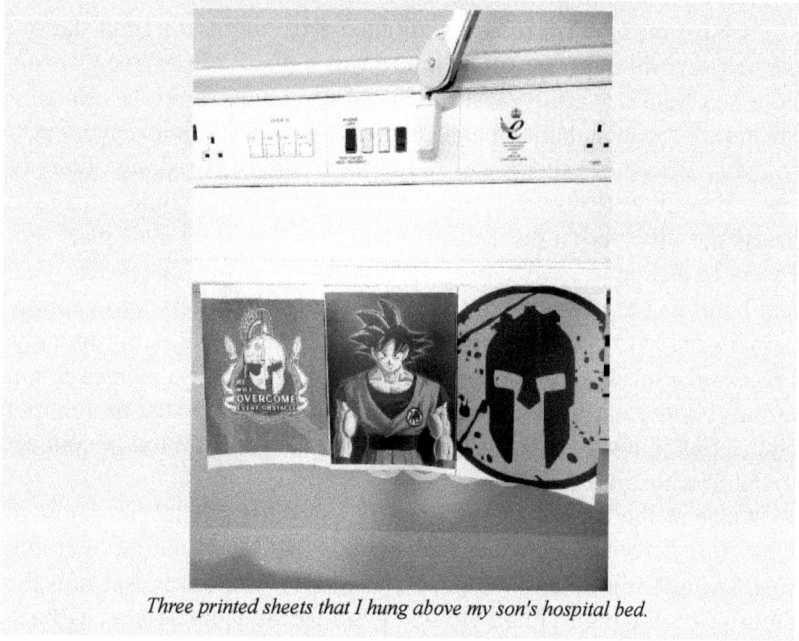

Three printed sheets that I hung above my son's hospital bed.

Plan for the next month

Your life only gets better when you get better.

Brian Tracy

A few more days had passed. We were gradually being introduced to how the intensive treatment would proceed, which was supposed to last for six months. Our son was still waiting for the procedure scheduled for the night of the twenty-fifth of February. The doctors' plan was that if the procedure succeeded, they would discharge the child home a few days later. The condition was that the test results had to be normal. If not, he would have to stay in the hospital.

Until the procedure, practically nothing had changed. Occasionally, I only had a delayed train, whether going or coming back. I continued to have my meals in the city. Every day, I brought Natalie to the hospital. There was even one day when there were no other patients in the room besides Sebastian. We were allowed to let Natalie visit her little brother. She was so thrilled to see him. It's indescribable. She sat next to him on the bed and, with her mother's help, hugged him. This help was necessary to avoid damaging the IV line from which medications were administered or for the child not to sit on the hand with the inserted catheters. We could enjoy that moment for less than an hour. Then, a nurse came to us and said that another patient was about to enter the room. They asked us to leave the place and go to the waiting room. The most important thing for us was that Natalie could see him at all, no matter how much time she spent with Sebastian. So I took the little one to the waiting room. Eve stayed with Sebastian. We tried to change every thirty minutes.

More days passed. Finally, the day came when our son was to undergo the procedure. Any form of general anesthesia always frightened us. We were also afraid of procedures. This was due to unpleasant past experiences during Natalie's treatment. Words like anesthesia or procedure had deeply rooted themselves in our minds. Unfortunately, the procedure couldn't be performed without anesthesia. We only prayed with my wife that everything would go smoothly. Without that, our son wouldn't be discharged home. He would have to stay in the hospital, and we didn't know for how long. Earlier, Natalie had undergone a series of surgeries. It was the first time for our son. We didn't even know how his body would react to anesthesia. There were many concerns. The hour was already late. I couldn't stay with Natalie in the hospital for too long. I just askedEveto keep me updated on the situation. When I was already at home, they took Sebastian to the operating room. Unfortunately, I don't remember how long the whole process took. I received the message that everything had gone according to plan from my wife only in the early morning. She also wrote to me that Sebastian was sleeping. She added that she was going to rest as well because she had had a sleepless night. The most important thing was that everything had worked out. With this thought, on my way to the platform, I stopped at a small shop where there was a coffee machine. I always took a hot drink in a double cup. I didn't have room for any beverage at Natalie's stroller. It was a stroller rented from the city authorities. However, they didn't have a cup holder in their offer. We had to buy most of the accessories out of our own pocket. Being on the platform, we had nothing else to do but wait for our means of transportation.

It was late February, and during this period, sunny days prevailed. Sometimes, I could even take off my jacket because it was getting too warm. After about fifteen minutes, I reached the hospital. My son was still sleeping. I sat down in a chair beside him and started sipping another cup of coffee that I had prepared in the hospital kitchen. I also grabbed two different flavored bars. 'Let him rest,' I thought, holding his hand. I had no intention of waking him up. Our shared playtime with building blocks and watching cartoons could wait. I took this moment to respond to all the messages people had sent me. Comments and shares on the fundraiser were steadily increasing. I glanced at the number of shares; it was already over fifty! It still hadn't sunk in for me that it was working. After maybe ten minutes, my own eyes began to close. The exhaustion was so overwhelming that my body was doing it automatically. At the same time, my son woke up. He didn't seem to notice that my eyes were half-closed. He handed me the TV remote, asking me to type in the name of the cartoon he wanted to watch at that moment. He loved it when I watched cartoons with him. On this day, the doctors were supposed to give us more information about our child's discharge from the hospital. However, no one showed up the entire day. We weren't surprised. We had often experienced the hospital staff saying one thing and doing another. I checked the time, and it was already late; I had to return home with Natalie. We said our goodbyes to the family and headed back on our monotonous route.

In the evening, as I sat at the computer, I was searching for information. I didn't know why so many people were having trouble making donations to the fundraiser. I couldn't find an answer to this question, but I came up with another idea. I did some research on the Internet and came across the website of an English foundation. You could create an account there, describe your case, and specify the amount you wanted to raise. This foundation deducted a commission from each transferred amount. I registered and shared the link to the website on my social media. In the description, I mentioned that many people had been unable to contribute to the previous fundraiser, so I had created an alternative option for them to try on this new website. Surprisingly, it took off instantly. The first donations started coming in. I was pleased that I had found a solution to the situation. I shut down the computer and went to sleep. The fatigue in my body was so strong that I fell asleep instantly.

The next day, while I was already at the hospital, the attending doctor entered the room. He said that the child would be discharged home the following day, provided we strictly followed a set of tasks. These tasks were crucial. We would also receive a printed A4 sheet with instructions on which medications to administer to the child and at what times. Everything would be detailed, including whether the medication should be taken before or after a meal and which syringes should we use, for which medications gloves are required, and so on... It was a substantial amount of information.

The most important thing, however, was that Sebastian would leave the hospital. The condition for discharging the child to home was his home isolation for a period of 6 weeks. The only exceptions would be the trips to the hospital for treatment. So, I brought as many things as I could manage back home with me. The rest would be brought by my wife on the day of our child's release. With so much baggage, I could barely make it back home. I wasn't entirely sure if we could handle it all, whether we would be able to keep up with all the medications. There were so many of them. One thing was certain, we had to face this new challenge.

My wife and I had decided that the next day I wouldn't go to the hospital but would instead prepare the house for their return. I turned on the TV for Natalie and started cleaning. Before putting little Natalie to bed, I played with her in her room. We played "store". She loved putting plastic fruits in a bag. When I asked her how much I should pay, she always answered, "five pounds." After an hour of play, I put the little one to sleep, gave her a kiss, and went downstairs to finish cleaning. The day flew by. As I was finishing up the dishes, I glanced at the clock in the kitchen. It was already late, so I sat on the couch. I wanted to take a short break and have some tea, but I ended up falling asleep.

When I woke up, it was already 3 in the morning. I took the cold tea back to the kitchen and went upstairs to check if our daughter was still asleep. I decided not to go back to bed. I turned on the computer and opened a file that had been waiting for a very long time to be finished. I had started writing a book about Natalie's story, but I never completed it. If you could assign icons to computer files based on how long they've been left untouched, this one would probably have cobwebs and a pile of dust on it. That's when I made the decision that this time, I would finish this incredible story and share it with the world. I began by reading what I had already written, which wasn't much, just under 40 pages in A5 format. After reading the text, I closed the computer. I had big ambitions. However, I didn't know if I would be able to revisit those memories. I told myself once more that this time, I would do everything in my power to complete this story.

As noon approached, I hadn't received any calls from my wife about when they would be back home. So, I decided to call her and ask if she had any news. She replied that everything was packed, and they were waiting for the discharge, but she didn't know how long it would take. She also mentioned that the hospital would arrange a taxi, and they would cover the cost. On one hand, I couldn't wait for my family to return home, but on the other hand, I was apprehensive about how it would be. It was already Monday, February 28.

Around 5:00 PM, I saw a taxi pull up outside the living room window. I helped my wife with the luggage, and then we led our child into the house, holding his hand. Sebastian seemed incredibly disoriented and exhausted. He didn't even greet me or his sister. He just sat down on the couch. He asked if I could hand him the game console controller, and I did without wanting to disturb him. I simply sat next to him. I was very glad that he was finally home. The day was coming to an end, and it was time to give the child his first medications on our own. Initially, my wife handled this task while I looked after our daughter.

A whole pack of blue medium-sized rubber gloves lay on the kitchen counter, next to the fridge. There was also a bag of syringes with different capacities. The medication schedule was prominently displayed. On another counter, this time near the water heater, there was a yellow bin for chemical waste. These new items in the kitchen took up a considerable amount of space, but the kitchen was the ideal place to keep all the chemicals away from the children. All the medications were prepared and mixed with unsweetened juice. Earlier, when Sebastian was still in the hospital, Eve had tried to give him the meds with water, but there was no way the child would take them that way.

It was truly a tough day for all of us. Sebastian's balance was compromised. Holding his left hand, I helped him climb the stairs. He gripped the handrail with his right hand. He took small, cautious steps along the path he could previously run up. The medication he was on was so strong that I had no idea how much it could disrupt his walking rhythm. It was evident that he was still sweating. Fortunately, he felt well enough not to vomit or develop a fever. He fell asleep instantly.

We didn't know what tomorrow would bring. We just wanted to get a good night's sleep. In the back of my mind, I had thoughts like: I hope Sebastian doesn't have to go back to the hospital, and I hope he doesn't feel unwell during the night. I fell asleep on the floor by his bed, holding his hand.

I woke up in the morning with a slight backache from the hard surface. When Sebastian heard me opening the gate we had installed at the top of the stairs, he woke up. He asked if I could help him get out of bed. He wanted to come downstairs with me and watch cartoons. Without hesitation, I turned around and helped him out of bed. He put on his slippers and carefully descended the stairs to the living room. I turned on the TV for him and went to the kitchen to prepare breakfast for everyone. Eve and Natalie were still asleep, and I made scrambled eggs with bacon and chives. Such a meal gave me energy for several hours.

As I heard the rest of the family waking up, I wondered when I would be able to resume my training. First, I had to adapt to my new responsibilities and then fit gym visits into the schedule.

Our home life had changed. Our son's diagnosis was a low blow. Even worse were the medications he received, particularly the steroids. Something dreadful. He was given a substantial dose, and the side effects included constant mood swings and growing aggression from day to day. Sometimes we couldn't calm him down, not even for 10 minutes. It was a nightmare, and it unfolded before the eyes of our little daughter.

Even if I wanted to hold him and comfort him, he would struggle as if caught in a trap, sometimes hitting and kicking wherever he could. He only calmed down when he ran out of energy to express his emotions and helplessness. Sometimes, my eyes welled up with tears. I didn't know how to help him in such situations.

The doctor told us that intensive treatment would last for six months, and we had to do our best to cope. If the aggression didn't subside, we might have to return to the hospital, which we desperately wanted to avoid. Days passed until Thursday approached, the day we had to go for another round of chemotherapy.

My New Responsibilities

Stress is resistance to what we don't want.

David R. Hawkins

On March 3rd, I woke up early, before everyone else. It was still dark outside. Our hospital appointment was scheduled for 10 o'clock, so I had plenty of time to get everything ready. I was most worried about the route. Due to our son's home isolation, this time I had to take the car. The worst part was the city center. Endless roadworks and lane changes paralyzed traffic every day. It was extremely stressful for me. I don't like situations where I have to change lanes suddenly and yield the right of way accidentally, and it has happened to me more than once. However, I was forced to overcome these fears and get to the hospital. If I had taken the train, Sebastian could easily catch an infection. His immune system was severely compromised, and we were not allowed to give him anything containing natural bacterial flora.

On that day, I told Eve that we had to leave earlier. So, I went outside to prepare the car, whose windows were frozen because the temperature was zero degrees outside. Wearing a winter hat and leather gloves, I used a special spray. It helped defrost the windows without the need for a scraper. Then, when the car was warm enough, we put the kids in their car seats in the back. I started the engine, and we set off on a journey that was supposed to take us 40 minutes. In practice, it took a bit longer.

The first traffic jam started just as we entered the highway, which was less than 5 minutes from our house. I lost about 6 minutes there. Then, when I got on the highway, I didn't have to wait long before another one began. This was all due to a wrecked car in the emergency lane. The police closed one lane, and the traffic flow only resumed after passing the patrol car. We were about 15 minutes behind schedule, and we hadn't even covered half of the distance. Thankfully, my previous experience taught me to leave with a significant time buffer. It reduced my stress level, although massive traffic jams only began after exiting the highway. The city was torn up wherever possible. Added traffic lights, speed limits, and speed cameras made our entire journey challenging.

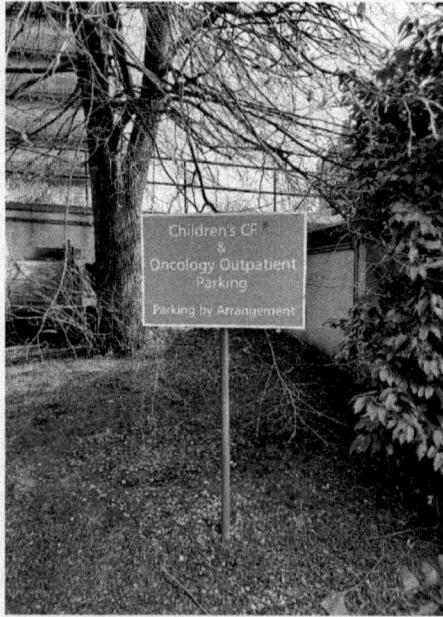

A sign indicating that the parking is for oncology patients only.

We reached our destination. We had a special ticket and a gate code for the oncology patients' parking. Our journey, instead of the planned 40 minutes, took over an hour. I unloaded Natalie's stroller from the trunk. We had agreed that I would take care of our daughter and go into the city to do some shopping, while Eve would take Sebastian for tests and call me when they were done so we could meet at the car. So, I took the little one with me and headed towards the crowded streets.

The crowds of people didn't allow me to move freely with the stroller on the sidewalk. Even though it was the beginning of March, there were an incredibly large number of people in the shopping center for this time of year. Sometimes I had to wait in line at the cash register for as long as 10 minutes, and it wasn't even a sale period.

I was wandering around the city with Natalie, not knowing which stores to enter anymore. Everything I needed to buy was already in bags and a backpack. I hadn't received any messages from my wife regarding our return. So, I sat on a metal bench in the center of the main street. A flock of pigeons gathered around the stroller, searching for scraps of food. Natalie, upon seeing the birds, got scared and started to cry. I reassured her, saying that animals are hungry too and that's how they search for food.

At that moment, the phone rang. Eve said that everything went according to plan, and we could slowly make our way back to the car. It took us 10 minutes to walk from the city center to the parking lot near the hospital. We met there. I could see that my wife was very tired. Sebastian also wanted to get in the car already.

As soon as I started the journey back, all the passengers fell asleep in the blink of an eye. They were sleeping so soundly that when I parked the car right in front of our home, I had to wake them up. I, sitting in the living room, took a half-hour nap. When I got up, I took my phone to check my social media. Everything had progressed so much that it exceeded my expectations. There were more and more shares and symbolic contributions. Lately, I had so much on my plate that I didn't have time to respond with thanks. I only did that in the evening when I was at my computer.

Once I finished responding, I started working on writing Natalie's history book further. I knew it would be a very tough journey. I had to recall all the details, mentally revisiting the places where death loomed over our heads, waiting only to take our daughter from us. Fortunately, the reaper lost the battle with us, and our little girl continues to delight in the smallest things to this day.

I opened my writing program. I took a deep breath, then slowly exhaled and began to continue this extraordinary story. Writing was incredibly difficult for me, so I decided that I would take it slowly. If I felt that I had already consumed too much stress recalling all the events on a given day, I would give up writing and start again when my emotions had subsided. That's exactly what I did that evening. I saved the file, then responded to a few more people who supported me in my fundraisers and went to bed.

My head was full of restless thoughts. I lay there, staring at the ceiling. I didn't know if I could finish this story. It was very hard for me to focus on writing while simultaneously recalling all the events related to my daughter.

The next day, we started by checking the child's temperature. We had our finger on the pulse. We realized that with such a low immune system, anything could happen. We always had the car ready, so we could go to the hospital immediately if needed. Every time we returned from the store, whether it was me or Eve, we thoroughly washed our hands to avoid bringing unnecessary germs near Sebastian. Isolation was like a prison for him. Sometimes he didn't know what to do with himself. Consoles, building blocks, and any other toys bored him, and you could see that he desperately wanted to go outside or meet friends. It broke my heart to see his suffering. Sometimes I shed a few tears. I was completely powerless in this matter. The only thing I could do was wait for this isolation to pass, and the child could go outside to get some fresh air. The only relief was the trips to the hospital, where he could briefly be outside.

Days went by. I could see that my wife was getting increasingly tired. We sat together in the living room after the children had already gone to sleep. We started discussing our responsibilities. We decided together that we would switch roles. Everything related to Sebastian will be on my shoulders, and Eve would take care of Natalie. We wanted to see if this solution would work better. We had to give it a try because the situation was becoming increasingly overwhelming.

The next day, Sebastian was bored. He looked out of his room window. He was upset that he couldn't go outside to play. His aggression began to escalate. The only thing we could do was wait or call the clinic. This would mean they would ask us to come to the ward immediately. We chose the first option. We waited for a while. The aggression subsided, but we didn't know for how long.

I continued to play with Sebastian with building blocks and small toy cars. In the evening, I had to learn how to administer home medications. I was scared, especially that I wouldn't remember all of them and the doses my son should receive. There were really a lot of medications during intensive treatment.

The time I had feared so much had come. Sebastian waited an hour after his last meal, and it was time to give him his first medication. I didn't have large gloves, so I used smaller ones. I put them on my large fingers, barely fitting. The next step was to shake the glass vial for 30 seconds. Then I opened a 5ml syringe, drew the medication, and poured it into a glass, mixing it with sugar-free juice (Sebastian didn't want to take any medications with water). He drank it. The next step was to give him the worst, in my opinion, medication, which was steroids. The procedure was similar, but without gloves and mixing the vial. On Mondays and Tuesdays, he also received a special antibiotic. It was a Tuesday, so I gave him that medication as well. After a while, the child went to sleep.

While in the kitchen, I grabbed the black pen pinned to the calendar. I circled the medications he received today. The paper was attached to the fridge, held in place by magnets from our vacations. On the upper left was Majorca, on the right was Sardinia, and in the middle at the bottom, there was a magnet from Wales. It was only after these procedures that I realized the new responsibilities that lay ahead of me. I was sure it wouldn't be easy, but I would do everything in my power to learn it all.

Sitting on the couch, I turned on my phone. I began responding to people's messages. I tried to do it as they came in. I didn't want the situation to accumulate so many messages that I wouldn't be able to reply to everyone. It already took me over an hour. One doesn't realize how many kind-hearted people there are until they find themselves in a critical situation.

After resting from a busy day, I went to the bedroom and fell asleep very quickly.

Locked in the house

Be strong. Don't be afraid to start working with what you have.
Don't be afraid to aim higher.

Regina Brett

Days passed. Sometimes it was sunny, and other times it rained. Occasionally, there was strong wind, but that wasn't important. What mattered more was when this darn isolation for Sebastian would end. There wasn't much time left now. More than half of this awful time had already passed. We couldn't wait for the day when our child could finally go outside, of course, gradually. The thought of how Sebastian would react to returning to his friends while on strong medication scared us.

March 10th was approaching. We lived between home and the hospital. We had a lot of visits with our son. Along the way, there were also visits with Natalie, but in a different hospital. I can confidently say that I knew almost every twist and turn in the corridors of both hospitals by heart. The schedule was extremely tight. On top of that, we had to be vigilant about hand hygiene to avoid bringing any germs home that could harm our son. We also had to watch the diets. We had to avoid any products that contained live bacterial cultures. These duties became easier from day to day, but the responsibility was very high.

One day, I received a call from a friend who lived in Scotland. He said that he would be in my area on March 15th and asked if he could come to visit the whole family. I told him that I needed to contact the clinic because our child was in home isolation. I had to find out first if it was safe. I said I would call him as soon as I got the information.

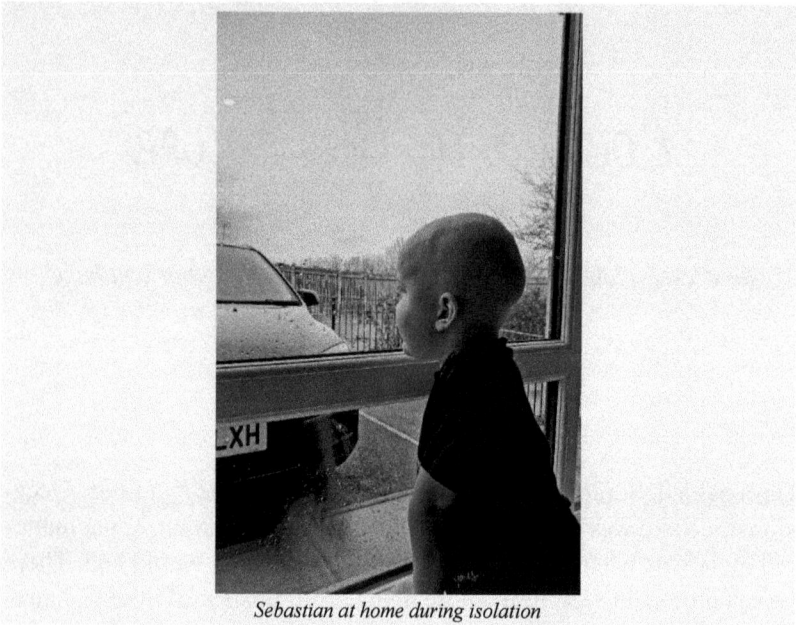

Sebastian at home during isolation

I called the oncology ward for information. We received a positive response in return. The condition was that only one person could visit,
and they had to observe proper hygiene precautions. The next day, I
called my friend and confirmed that he could come. I was in a shopping
center in Leeds at the time, and shortly after I finished the call, another
person called me. He lived in the south of England. He said he would
be in the area on March 16th and asked if it was possible to visit my
family. With the information from the clinic that such a possibility exi-
sted, I confirmed the visit. We agreed to meet on Wednesday in the
afternoon. I was very surprised. My friends reached out to me, wanting
to visit us, knowing what we were currently going through. From the
influx of information, I completely forgot that on March 17th, my mom
was supposed to visit us and that in the evening of that day, I was supposed to pick her up from the Manchester airport. To ensure that I wouldn't forget anything, I took a notebook. I wrote down all the important dates so I wouldn't have to think about them.

The next days passed without any changes. Finally, Wednesday came, the day of the first visit. We explained to our son that a certain gentleman would be coming to visit today. Hours passed, Sebastian gazed out the window in anticipation of the guest. Finally, the moment arrived. A silver BMW parked right next to our Ford Focus. We had space for two cars in the driveway, so there was no problem with parking. We welcomed Michael. We sat in the living room with coffee and cake. Sebastian and Natalie received gifts, which they were very pleased with.

Together with my friend, we thought about how to increase the reach of the fundraisers I was organizing even more. After some time, we found a way that, as it turned out later, worked. About 4 hours passed, and Michael had to head back home. A long journey awaited him back to Scotland. We thanked him for the visit, the words of support, and for helping with the fundraiser algorithms. We were very pleased to have so many kind-hearted people among us.

Thursday arrived. A beautiful sunrise promised good weather for the entire day. Unfortunately, we couldn't go for a walk with the kids yet. Well, we could with Natalie, but for Sebastian, to avoid upsetting him, we simply didn't consider it.

During breakfast, our son began asking about the next guest and when his grandmother would arrive. The child, still on medication all the time, was still sweating. We had to change his clothes at least twice a day. Just like yesterday, Sebastian gazed out the window, awaiting the person who would soon arrive. This time, an Infinity car parked in our parking lot. As we did yesterday, we welcomed the guest and sat down with coffee and tea to talk. Paul is a very good person. His words of support during his visit added even more motivation for us to act. The visit lasted only about two hours because our friend had a long way home. When he left, Sebastian continued to look out the window, but this time it was already dark. It was truly a beautifully spent time.

In the evening, my wife and I spent our time watching one of our favorite series when the kids were already asleep. I couldn't wait for the next day. One of the most important women in my life, my mother, was coming to visit us. We continued watching the series. I don't remember when I fell asleep.

I woke up the next morning with my head on the pillow and a blanket on the couch. I must have been very tired since I didn't wake up during the night to go to bed. I got up feeling refreshed, with a slightly numb hand that I had positioned in an awkward way. A few movements up and down, and my hand quickly returned to normal, leaving a slight tingling sensation for a while.

To pick up my mom from the airport, I had to wait until the evening. The flight was very late, and the plane was landing around 11 PM. The day passed without any changes. In the evening, I got in the car and set out on the journey to Manchester airport. I enjoyed driving on the highway, although I was alone with songs playing from the CD. I definitely preferred to have good company when I was driving, rather than having no one to talk to.

I arrived at the first terminal. My mom was already waiting. It turned out that the plane arrived 30 minutes earlier. She got into the car, and I greeted a very important person to me. We set off on the way back home. I started telling her everything. As we approached the exit onto the highway, it turned out that it was closed due to roadworks. I pulled over on the first possible shoulder. I took my phone and started looking for an alternative route. We drove through villages that were poorly lit. On the way back, I told my mom that I had started writing a book about Natalie's history. I added that this time I would succeed, and the book would be published. My mom was very supportive of this project. She knew her granddaughter's story very well. We arrived home an hour later than planned. The most important thing was that we arrived safely. Eve was still awake. She greeted her mother-in-law and then the three of us sat down for tea. Our conversations continued almost until 1 in the morning.

The next day, Sebastian came downstairs with my help. I had to hold his hand to prevent him from falling. He looked at his grandmother and greeted her from a distance. He had a sad expression. I didn't know what the reason was. I could only guess that it was a side effect of steroids or some other medication.

Over time, our son warmed up to his grandmother and came to hug her. The day before, we had decided that my mom would stay with the kids at home in the evening, and Eve and I would go on a date to take a break from our daily duties.

We went to the movies to see "My Debt". Then, we went to a café that also served delicious desserts. It was located in the same building as the cinema. We had a great time and returned home.

My mom's visit lasted for 3 days. When we said goodbye, we thanked her from the bottom of our hearts for the visit. I also told her that I would keep her updated on the situation so she wouldn't worry. Once she headed towards her terminal, I set out on the journey back home. This time, however, they didn't close the entrance to the highway for me.

My wife and I at a dessert café after watching the movie "My Debt".

Two different worlds

Don't wait. The time will never be just right.

Napoleon Hill

The end of March was approaching. As I was going through my phone, I received a message from a friend. She had heard about what had happened to us and wanted to help in any way possible. I thanked her because any help in such a difficult life situation was much appreciated. She replied that we would stay in touch, wishing us a great day nonetheless.

In the meantime, I was traveling with Sebastian for chemotherapy in Leeds, while Eve was taking care of Natalie and her rehabilitation. Our daughter had occasional ultrasound scans of various organs to ensure that her development was progressing well. With a spina bifida, there was a significant risk of internal organ damage, especially the kidneys. If Natalie's catheterization wasn't successful, urine could back up into her kidneys. Therefore, this organ was closely monitored by the doctors. Fortunately, the follow-up examinations went well, and we had nothing to worry about.

One evening, as I was getting ready for bed, I received another message from my friend. She informed me that she would be organizing a charity fancy dress ball for children, and asked if April 16th worked for us to attend. I checked my calendar and had an opening. Our son's isolation would be over by that date, so we could confidently go as a whole family. I confirmed the date.

My friend also mentioned that on April 2nd, I should come to the town of Barnsley, around midnight. I scratched my head because I had no idea what she was talking about. It wasn't until a moment later that I received another message, explaining that there was a club there where they held concerts. But that wasn't the important part. The main idea was to sell raffle tickets, and the prize was a bottle of rum. All the money from ticket sales would be donated to us. I was surprised but agreed to go. The city was just under 20 minutes away by car, so it wasn't far. However, I was worried about something else. However, something else concerned me. How will I find my way there if it's completely not my world? How could I go on stage without being overwhelmed by stage fright and draw the raffle numbers into the microphone? I had to face it and just go there. I still had some time to prepare if needed.

After the conversation with my friend, I went to sleep, while my wife continued to browse information about Natalie's rehabilitation that we received from the physiotherapist. We all wanted Natalie to be as independent as possible.

Time passed quickly, and before I knew it, it was April 2nd. By that time, we had placed collection tins in stores with invitations to the children's ball. In some shops, posters were also hung up. We wanted the event to be as well-publicized as possible. Sebastian had started his console early in the morning, and I went to the kitchen to prepare breakfast. Fried eggs with bacon were one of our favorite dishes. I added finely chopped chives to my plate, but Sebastian wasn't a fan of them.

A smile would appear on my face every time I saw Sebastian eat. The doctors said that the child should eat, no matter what kind of food, as long as he ate. If he didn't (and with this condition, there are many children who have no appetite), Sebastian would have to have a nasal tube - a white tube through which he would be fed.

We finished. Sebastian went back to playing on his console, and I called my workplace. The company's policy was that I had to go there from time to time (usually about every 2 weeks) to report on the situation. I scheduled the meeting for 10 o'clock and drove there. While waiting in the cafeteria, I ran into some acquaintances. Some greeted me and asked how I was holding up. I had a fairly long conversation with one colleague. After a while, the manager arrived. We went to another room so that I could provide the information. That day, I had another medical leave certificate with me, which was issued for 3 months.

After handling the formalities, I drove back home. Even though I lived very close, the return trip took me even longer this time. Additional traffic lights at the intersection and road construction caused a significant traffic jam.

I returned home. When I opened the door, the children were smiling. Sebastian quickly ran over to hug me. Natalie, as quickly as she could, crawled over on her knees. It was clear to the naked eye that the children needed me at home now. Going back to working in the warehouse was not possible at all. At that moment, I deeply considered what I could do to be able to give up fundraising and start supporting myself in a different way. I was in the process of writing a book, but I didn't know if I would be able to support myself from it after it was published.

The day was coming to an end. The sun had set, and stars began to appear in the clear sky. It was a full moon. Glancing at my phone, I was waiting for a message from my friend. She was supposed to let me know the exact time to arrive at the club. Even though this club was intended for a specific subculture, I dressed normally. I didn't have colorful hair, leather jackets with patches, earrings, or tattoos. I didn't smoke, and I drank alcohol very sporadically. I also listened to different music. For me, these were two different worlds. I had no idea how to fit in.

Around 9 PM, my phone rang. I received instructions to arrive before midnight because the award presentation was scheduled to take place during the break between two artists who were performing at the club that day. So, I did just that. I parked my car near the club entrance and opened the door. Inside, there was a choking cloud of cigarette smoke. My eyes started to sting a little, and I looked for my friend. Heavy music was playing on the stage, and people were dancing while making various hand gestures. I found her, greeted her, and shortly after, her partner said to me, "Welcome to my world." It was so loud inside that we had to step out into the corridor so she could give me the details. She explained that she had sold a large number of lottery tickets, and I was supposed to go on stage precisely at midnight after being announced by the host. In addition to the tickets, she also had a large piece of rolled-up paper. I asked her, "What's this?" She replied that it was a big poster I should take with me when I go back home. The poster was related to another charity event for Sebastian, scheduled for April 16th at a hall near the church in Barnsley. I thanked her and took the poster to my car to ensure it wouldn't get damaged. I returned to the smoky hall, waiting until midnight.

Time passed quickly. Finally, the moment arrived. I swallowed saliva. The host called me onto the stage. The music fell silent. I ascended the small steps onto the stage, standing next to the microphone. Hundreds of people were looking at me, waiting for me to say something. After a moment, I spoke.

First, I thanked everyone for participating in the lottery, explaining how much it meant to me. Then, I yelled into the microphone at the top of my lungs, "Who's ready for the lottery?!" In response, I heard positive reactions. I also noticed that some people were raising beer bottles. I reached into the box. Opening a piece of paper folded into four parts, the number 48 was revealed. I shouted that number 48 had won! Silence fell. No one spoke. I repeated it two more times, but the lucky winner was not in the room. The host came on stage and said that in this case, I would draw another number. This time it was 54. The lucky winner came on stage to claim her prize, and the crowd began to clap and whistle. The music started playing again, and the host announced the next concert. After leaving the stage, I wiped the sweat from my forehead. A friend told me I did great. I thanked her for everything but had to head home. It was very late, and I had to get up early in the morning. I promised her that I would tally everything and let her know the total amount raised.

When I got back home, the smell of cigarettes was noticeable, even though I didn't smoke myself. My clothes had absorbed the smell, so I quickly threw them in the laundry and then went to take a shower. It was an incredible experience. I was so tired that I can't remember when I fell asleep. I was only woken up in the morning by the alarm set for 6 o'clock.

While sipping my morning coffee, I wondered how to motivate myself to write a book. I was also concerned about the fact that in creating it, I would have to revisit all those painful moments. I wanted this book to tell the true story of my daughter, straight from my heart.

I finished the last sip of black coffee and remembered that I left a poster in the car that a friend had given me. So, I quickly went to get it. I unraveled it, undoing the two blue rubber bands. It was quite large. I started to think about where I could place it, but nothing came to mind.

I called my wife and asked if she had any ideas. She suggested taking it to Sebastian's school. Perhaps some children who knew him would want to come to the event dressed as their favorite characters.

This idea seemed excellent to me. One question came to mind, though: where would we put the poster if the school didn't want to accept it? Eve replied not to worry about it, but to simply take it to the school's reception first and ask.

I went to the bathroom to freshen up a bit. Despite having already taken a shower, I still smelled of cigarettes on my skin.

I got in the car and drove to the school. A young woman working at the reception opened a small window, pressing a tiny handle. She asked how she could help. I explained everything to her. They were happy to take the poster. They knew what had happened to Sebastian, whom they knew well from school. They confirmed that the poster would hang in the school corridor.

I thanked them from the bottom of my heart and returned home. I was starting to get hungry; I hadn't eaten anything since morning, aside from drinking coffee.

On the same day, Eve received a phone call from Sebastian's school with a proposal. Specifically, the school declared that they would also hold a charity event for our son, and on April 29th, children would come to school dressed as their favorite characters. The very kind lady on the phone also mentioned that they would organize a lottery, and the funds raised from ticket sales would go towards helping Sebastian. The only thing the school needed was our approval.

We didn't have to think about the decision for long. Without hesitation, we confirmed that the school had our permission to organize the event.

I was in shock. I had never imagined that since I made the decision to do everything in my power to help my son, the response would be so overwhelming.

End of imprisonment

If you can dream it, you can do it.

Walt Disney

We used to go to the hospital every Thursday. As I mentioned earlier, in the beginning, my wife used to go to the clinic with Sebastian. However, now I have taken over all the responsibilities, including taking our son for check-ups. It was the first time it was my turn.

I took the elevator to the C floor. Walking down the winding corridor, I reached the pediatric oncology ward. I pressed the intercom and then headed towards the reception. Once the formalities were completed, we sat in the waiting room, and people started to arrive. Some children had nasal tubes. You could also see children in wheelchairs and some without hair. Once again, I realized that such things happen. It really hits a person when you find yourself in such a place.

Sebastian sat next to me. Snuggled up against me, he watched cartoons on a tablet connected to the hospital's free internet. At first, the child was called in for measurements and weighing, and then he was to return to the waiting room and wait for the doctor. About 30 minutes passed. We were called in by the doctor, and we went to his office. The doctor entered everything I said into the computer. How the child feels, how we are managing at home, and so on... The doctor said that all this data is very important so they can help us as much as possible. Based on the blood test results, medication doses were adjusted.

After the consultation, we returned to the waiting room. This time, we were waiting for the nurse to administer chemotherapy through the port. In the meantime, a man with a folder full of various documents approached us. He introduced himself and said he was here to help families with all the paperwork related to benefits. This was his specialty. I called Eve to discuss the offer. With so much on our plate, we also decided to take advantage of this help. We arranged for him to come to our home and assist us with everything. All the official paperwork was complete magic to us.

We left the clinic after about 3 hours. We went straight to the car, waiting for Eve and Natalie to return from the city. It was the end of the isolation period. On one hand, we were happy that it was ending, but on the other hand, we were worried about how our child would readjust to the world he used to live in before his illness. While driving home, these thoughts troubled me. Once again, all the passengers in the car fell asleep after an intense day, and I safely reached our destination.

The home visit was scheduled for Monday, so we had three more days ahead of us. Isolation was supposed to end on Sunday. Then, taking advantage of the nice weather they forecasted, we wanted our son to go out for at least an hour in front of the house to get some fresh air.

The following days passed very similarly to the previous ones until the moment we had been waiting for finally arrived. We woke up on Sunday morning. The first thing I did was check my phone to see what the weather forecast was for the afternoon. It was supposed to be clear skies and sunny, although the temperature was expected to be around 10 degrees.

The morning flew by quickly. After lunch, we set up our garden chairs in front of the house. Sebastian took his scooter and was very happy to finally be able to leave the house. The end of imprisonment had come! For a moment, I wondered what was worse, the 6-week isolation of our son or the steroids he was receiving? It was hard to find an answer to that. I hoped that every day from now on would be better, and that we would fight this damn leukemia as quickly as possible!

We sat in front of the house, savoring every minute and watching Sebastian's smile. Natalie was with us as well. She sat on a mat, drawing colorful doodles on the asphalt. On the first day, we didn't want to overdo it, so as planned, we returned home after an hour. I sat down with my son at the console, and Eve took care of the little one and her rehabilitation exercises.

Monday came. The person I had met at the clinic was supposed to arrive shortly. While waiting, I had a cup of instant coffee, and then I heard the sound of a parking car. Once our guest entered the house, we sat in the kitchen, and a very large stack of papers was pulled out of the folder. I can't recall how many documents we had to present, filling out everything on the forms. It took quite a while. Finally, we managed to complete all the pages. The next step was to send them to the office and wait for a response.

In the meantime, we were presented with an offer for a trip. It turned out that in Wales, they rent cottages for families whose children have been diagnosed with cancer. Everything was to be covered by the foundation, and our only expense was getting there. We didn't fill out this offer yet. We took the papers. We wanted to review the offer calmly. Today, we had already had enough of scribbling with pens. The stack of documents was overwhelming. Filling out paperwork for the office was not our strong suit at all. Fortunately, there was a person who helped us complete it. He also declared that we could count on him for future documents. We thanked him very warmly for his assistance. As he left on his way back, Sebastian looked out the window, and the sun was beginning to set.

Both my wife and I were tired and pleased that everything was starting to go in the right direction. Today, however, the most important thing was that Sebastian's isolation was finally over. We could now calmly begin planning his return to social life.

We were somewhat worried about how our son would adapt to school after such a long break. He really wanted to go back to his peers. We had no choice but to wait for when it would be possible. While his isolation had ended, he could only return to school on April 25th.

We also spent the next day in front of the house. The weather was very nice, and there wasn't a cloud in the sky.

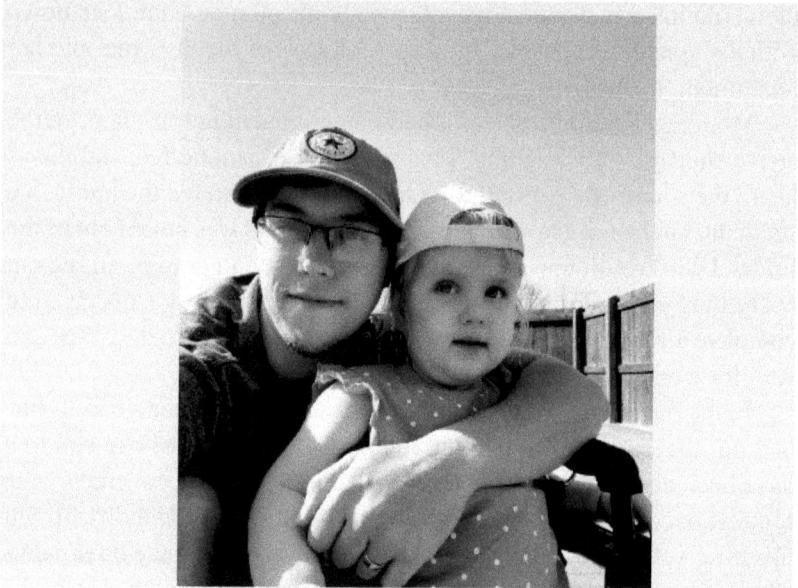

My daughter and I during outdoor rehabilitation exercises in front of the house

Fancy dress party

Life is like riding a bicycle. To keep your balance, you must keep moving.

Albert Einstein

When I had a hearty breakfast, I found a moment to reply to everyone and thank them for their donations to the fundraiser I was organizing. There were quite a lot of them. I carefully reviewed everything to avoid accidentally missing anyone. Funds were coming in almost every day, and the fundraiser was approaching the limit I had set. Thanks to this money, my wife and I could focus on our son's treatment without worries. All the funds were constantly allocated for hospital trips, hygiene products (because Sebastian sweated quickly), clothes that we couldn't keep up with washing, and so on. One thing was certain: without the help of kind-hearted people, it would have been very difficult for me to face my son's illness.

Day by day, I became a different person. My self-confidence grew very quickly, and matters that were once stressful and unattainable to me became trivial.

The day of the charity event was approaching. Sebastian had a choice of several different costumes to dress up in. He couldn't decide which one to choose. With Eve's help, we assisted him in making a selection. Eventually, our son decided to dress up as Superman. The blue suit with a red cape suited him perfectly. Sebastian asked us if his school friends would come to the party. We couldn't answer that question. I told him, squatting beside him, that we would see, but I had a feeling that someone would definitely come. My intuition suggested so.

We didn't have a costume for Natalie. An alternative solution was that a face painter was confirmed for the party. She specialized in making face paintings for children. So we decided that once we were there, we would ask the artist to paint ladybugs on Natalie's face because she really liked them.

I sent a message to a friend who was one of the event organizers. We agreed on the time we should arrive. We were supposed to come early to prepare everything before the guests arrived. We got the kids ready and set off.

Being close to the destination, my GPS failed me. It showed a completely different location. After a moment, I found a parking spot to call my friend and ask for directions to the specific address. Fortunately, after so many years in the UK, my English was good enough to communicate without any problems in a foreign language. We arrived. We parked the car in a tiny parking lot near the church. Our friend hadn't arrived yet, but she was expected to be there any moment.

We entered the room, looking around to see how large it was. After a moment, a very friendly gentleman, one of the organizers, welcomed us. He showed us where the kitchen was and pointed out the storage room from which we were to take out the folding chairs. But before I started getting the chairs, I brought Natalie's walker from the car so she could move around on the dance floor.

The preparations continued. We put together four tables to display the prizes for the raffle. There was so much food that we were sure it would be enough for everyone. I still couldn't believe that once again I found myself in a place I never expected to be. Since I made the decision to help my family as best as I could, new opportunities had opened up before me.

It was 2 o'clock. Guests slowly started to arrive, greeting us. Most of them asked how Sebastian was feeling and wished him a speedy recovery.

Music was playing from two large speakers. Children were running around the whole room, goofing off. Adults formed smaller groups, discussing topics of interest to them. Sebastian and Eve sat at a table, then started selling raffle tickets. Children would come by the booth, looking at the prizes. There were various books, pencil cases, crayons, markers, and many other interesting prizes to be won. Each time a child dropped money into our donation jar, Sebastian would draw a number from a silver pot where the tickets were placed. I was keeping an eye on Natalie during this time. Since she was in the walker, she was more vulnerable, and there was a chance that a child might not notice her and bump into her.

Other event hosts brought cake and other sweets. Next to the drink station, a second raffle was set up. This one was aimed at the adults, with the main prize being a large bottle of wine.

The entire ball was supposed to end at 4 o'clock. Time was passing quickly. People slowly started to disperse. I, myself, was very tired. With so many responsibilities, I wasn't getting enough sleep. Even though I drank a few cups of coffee a day, I still felt like I was running low on energy. I started to wonder how I could manage it, but I couldn't come up with any solutions. The children often woke up during the night, which disrupted my sleep pattern.

When there were just a few people left in the room before the event ended, we began cleaning up slowly. I was pleased with the outcome of the event. I told a friend who was one of the organizers that I would count the money raised at home as soon as possible and let her know the total amount.

I picked up Sebastian, and he fell asleep in my arms. The medication he was taking was greatly weakening him.

It was time for us to return home. We wholeheartedly thanked all the organizers for creating such a wonderful charity event. I personally thanked the guests as they left the room.

As we left the church parking lot, Eve and I waved goodbye to everyone.

Back to School

When you're going through some hard times and wonder where God is, remember the teacher is always quiet during a test.

Keanu Reeves

Days went by until the long-awaited day finally arrived. Sebastian, after a very long break, could return to school. So, I took out his school uniform from his black dresser: dark gray pants along with a red sweatshirt, underneath which was an elegant white shirt. The red and gray tie also looked perfect. When I buttoned the first button of his shirt, I saw a smile on his face. He was very happy to be able to go back to his peers, even for the few hours set in the school schedule. Week by week, the hours of the child's presence at school were to increase, and Sebastian was to be observed on how he was coping.

I got into the car and waited for my son, who gave a kiss to Eve before saying goodbye. Through the slightly open window, I heard my wife telling him not to worry and that everything would be fine. Sebastian got into the car with a joyful expression. As I started driving, he waved to his mom, and she reciprocated with the same gesture.

There were still 20 minutes until the start of the lessons. I always arrived early at the small parking lot located behind the bus stop. If I arrived 10 minutes later, it would already be full. I don't like being late, especially in such an important matter for my son. So, taking advantage of the nice weather, we approached the green school gate. We had to wait for the school janitor to open it so we could enter the school grounds. It didn't take long. The gate was opened, and Sebastian began to look slowly for his classmates. He recognized a few faces. Children approached him, welcoming him back. The bell rang, and all the students lined up, waiting for the teacher.

I said goodbye to Sebastian, giving him a high five. I told him I'd pick him up in the reception area shortly. I went back home and told Eve how our son was welcomed by his peers.

I took a short nap. Eve woke me up, saying it was time to go and pick up Sebastian from school. I looked at the clock, still half-asleep. I couldn't believe how quickly time had passed. Apparently, I was so tired that I overslept those few hours.

When I picked up Sebastian from school, I saw a smile on his face. He told me he wanted to stay longer in class. I replied that it would be possible with time, but we needed to wait a little longer. We returned home. After greeting his mom and sister, Sebastian sat on the couch and started playing his favorite console game, Crash Bandicoot.

I, on the other hand, went to the kitchen. I had to regularly check the status of the medications Sebastian was taking. The dosages varied depending on the weekly blood test results. The primary medications our son was taking were Mercaptopurine, Methotrexate, and Co-trimoxazole. When Sebastian started a new cycle of treatment, he also took steroids for 5 days. During that time, we had to watch him closely as he became aggressive after taking them. It broke my heart every time I saw him so angry. I felt helpless and couldn't do anything. If the aggression escalated, the doctors said we would need to go to the clinic. What's more, my wife and I kept a close eye on him all the time. A fever of 38 degrees or more was enough to land us in the hospital.

Fortunately, it hadn't happened so far. However, we were aware that it might happen sooner or later. On the way, we had to remember all the additional preparations in case of a sudden trip to the clinic, such as a fully fueled car or a packed hospital bag in the closet.

The day was slowly coming to an end. Time was passing quickly, and I was wondering what would happen next. I was still waiting for a response from the authorities regarding the highest level of disability allowance for my son. Unfortunately, bureaucratic matters take a long time, especially when your application is rejected, and you have to appeal, which has happened to us multiple times when applying for a disability allowance for Natalie.

However, this time all the paperwork was filled out by a specialist, so there was a very high chance that the application would be approved on the first try.

Friday, April 29th arrived. On this day, another charity event was scheduled, this time at the school Sebastian attended.

The day before, I had taken my son to Leeds for chemotherapy. The procedure had left him very tired. We were unsure whether to allow him to go to the ball or just take him to school when the prize drawing would happen. The lottery was set to take place an hour before the end of the regular school day in a large sports hall.

We talked to our son. Rubbing his tired eyes, he said he wanted to go to school and be present for the prize distribution. He also mentioned that he wanted to dress up as Superman again.

Eve and I agreed that if necessary, I would pick him up from school earlier.

Sebastian had a very good day at school. When I picked him up, he was disappointed that he couldn't stay longer. Unfortunately, his return to school was planned gradually. The only consolation for him was the knowledge that we would return later in the day to see the prize distribution. The main prize was a mountain bike.

We returned home. The weather outside was beautiful. The sun was shining brightly, and there wasn't a cloud in the sky.

We all sat down at the table for lunch. Sebastian kept checking the clock. He couldn't wait for the moment when we would go back to school for the second time. He was incredibly impatient. Even after coming back from school, he didn't want to change out of his Superman outfit; he wanted to wear it the whole time.

Finally, he got his wish. I hadn't even finished putting on my shoes, and Sebastian was already waiting by the car. We dressed Natalie and headed to the school.

In the sports hall, we took seats in the back row. We didn't expect that so many parents would be there 30 minutes before the event started. The school had put a lot of effort into organizing it. On the stage, you could see a large number of prizes, a microphone, and a big screen. Besides the main prize, the large pink teddy bear on the left side really caught my attention. It was genuinely funny. I wondered how the winner would take it home. Everyone was waiting for the event to begin. After a moment, a woman from the school approached the microphone and introduced herself. She also brought a box with tickets. Looking around, I saw that almost everyone in the audience was already holding their tickets and eagerly awaiting the reading of their numbers.

The raffle began. First, smaller prizes were awarded, and in the end, the largest ones. Only the main prize was left. The crowd watched a piece of paper folded into four parts. The number was read out, and the lucky winner received the mountain bike. Everyone around started applauding, not just for the person who won but also for the school for organizing such a fantastic event.

I was moved. Through teary eyes, I once again realized that my determination was yielding very good results. I was proud of the fact that I was doing my best and not giving up in situations where obstacles were thrown in my path. I fight, no matter what!

One of the teachers asked us to stay after everyone had left the hall. The school representatives told us that they would count the money collected and inform the school of the total amount raised. The entire fundraiser was to be divided. Part of the funds would be transferred to my foundation account, while the other part would go to the hospital where Sebastian was being treated.

Our whole family expressed our gratitude for such a wonderful gesture.

Scooter Rally

The whole secret of a successful life is to find out what is one's destiny to do, and then do it.

Henry Ford

May arrived. The sun's rays brightened our living room, and I headed to the kitchen to prepare breakfast. Instinctively, I reached for the kettle and set it to boil water for coffee. As I turned on the gas stove, I contemplated the future of our family. I could take sick leave from work until at most August 10th. By then, I had to decide whether to return to work or not. We hadn't received any answers from the authorities regarding Sebastian's benefits. Time was running out, and the stress associated with it was increasing for me.

Writing a book about Natalie's history was progressing slowly. First, due to a lack of time, and second, it was very challenging to revisit those events in my mind. However, I knew that her story was valuable and worth publishing. It would help parents in similar situations, like we once were, make the right decisions. One of the most challenging aspects of creating it was not writing the text but going through archival photos. Looking at them made me feel as if I were there at that moment.

We lived in a peaceful neighborhood. One day, while Sebastian was playing outside with his friends, a neighbor approached me. He asked if I'd like him to organize a scooter rally. Most of the scooter club members would come with their machines to our house. He also wanted the proceeds from this rally to go toward helping Sebastian.

I was surprised and didn't know how to respond. Once again, people with kind hearts appeared on my path. Such moments were genuinely uplifting for me. I was pleased that the effort my wife and I put in to help our children as much as possible was yielding such positive results.

I agreed. I thanked him with a firm handshake for his help. We mutually agreed on the date for May 12th in the afternoon.

When my son finished playing outside with his friends, we returned home. Natalie was having her rehabilitation exercises at that time. Of course, after she finished, she would also go outside to play. I asked Eve if there was any way I could help her during the exercises with our daughter. She thanked me but preferred that I check the status of the medications and syringes. If something was running low, I was to make a note in a notebook, and then, during our Thursday visit to the oncology clinic, request the necessary items. At home, we were running out of syringes of various capacities and blue disposable gloves. I looked at the box. There weren't too many syringes left. A pack of gloves stood nearby. Their supply should last for at least another two weeks. I wrote down in the notebook everything that needed to be taken from the clinic.

Sebastian was still undergoing intensive treatment, which was supposed to conclude after 6 months. We were about halfway through this period. The doctors assured us that as this time passed, we would need to go to the hospital less frequently. There would no longer be a need for weekly visits. Undoubtedly, the intensive treatment was the most challenging stage of the battle against cancer. I remained patient with Eve. I knew that time would pass regardless. At that moment, however, I focused more on helping my family as best as I could.

As I sat lost in thought in the kitchen, Sebastian approached me. He asked if I wouldn't go and play with him in his room upstairs. He didn't want to play outside anymore. Apparently, he was tired enough to prefer being at home. I replied that I would, but first, I needed to help Mom dress Natalie. Our daughter had finished her exercises and also wanted to go outside. While I put Natalie's shoes on, Sebastian tugged at my shirt, asking me to come and play with him. I couldn't blame him for such behavior. It was evidently a side effect of the medications he was taking. Such behavior hadn't occurred with him earlier. In particular, the steroids he was taking periodically showed how much they could change someone's character. A short moment passed. Natalie went outside with Mom, and I went upstairs to Sebastian's room.

The next day, I received information that approximately 50 people were likely to attend the scooter rally scheduled for tomorrow.

I informed all the neighbors that a charity event was being organized for tomorrow. I also added that it might get quite loud and apologized in advance for it.

Sebastian couldn't wait anymore. He had never seen so many scooters in one place in his entire life! He was very excited. From his room, he had a view of the neighborhood street where those machines were going to be parked tomorrow.

I was awakened from my sleep this time, not by the alarm clock. Sebastian stood next to me and nudged my arm. Through sleepy eyes, I asked him what was going on and why he had gotten up so early. In response, he said he couldn't wait for the scooters to arrive in our neighborhood. I looked out the window. The sun was just rising, and the clock showed 5 o'clock. I got out of bed and hugged my son very tightly. I was also delighted with his happiness. To see that, despite his illness, he could still enjoy life.

I went to the kitchen to prepare breakfast for him. Despite the early hour, he was very hungry.

On that day, in addition to the event, we also had an appointment at the oncology clinic. I had the meeting time noted in the calendar for 10 AM. After enjoying delicious scrambled eggs with bacon, we went to the living room to play video games. Natalie and Eve were still asleep. We didn't want to wake them up, so we closed the living room door. Sebastian loved playing with me. We still had an hour before the train. We played racing games, and Sebastian won, laughing that he had beaten Dad once again. The smile never left his face. Time passed quickly. We turned off the console and went to catch the train.

Whenever we were very close to the entrance to the small train station in our town, I read the information board. The display showed the schedule of the respective train. Fortunately, ours was on time. Traveling on these lines, trains often ran late. Unfortunately, apart from our car, this was the only direct connection between our town and Leeds.

We left the clinic quite quickly. Sebastian received another dose of chemotherapy. We picked up the necessary medications and accessories, such as syringes or disposable gloves, before heading back home.

We had lunch. There were still a few hours left until the scooter rally. Since the weather was very nice, we went outside. Sebastian took a ball with him. We gave Natalie a baby walker, so she could exercise outdoors. She also brought along a much smaller ball.

While playing ball with my son, I received a message. It said that everyone was already on their way and should be here any moment. I took the ball back to the house. I stood in a safe place with Sebastian, and Eve went home with Natalie. We were expecting a lot of noise, and Natalie didn't have earmuffs. She was afraid of loud sounds. Just a fast train passing only through our train station was enough to make her cry.

We waited. Most of our friends who lived nearby also came out in front of their houses. Sebastian stayed close to me, and in the distance, you could hear the revving of engines.

The sound intensified with each passing second. Suddenly, scooters started coming down from around the corner. There were so many of them that I couldn't count them all! Owners of classic machines parked them wherever they found a little free space. Various symbols, flags, and additional headlights were attached to the scooters. Most people who came had club jackets with different patches. Kids walked from scooter to scooter, admiring and marveling at them.

Suddenly, our neighbor, the organizer of the entire event, approached Sebastian. He gave him gifts and a model to place on the desk. It was an old, blue Italian scooter. It had the Italian flag with the word ROMA painted on the front. It also had a swivel handlebar so that it could be displayed in any position. After a moment, a man approached Sebastian and asked if he would like to sit on his scooter. Sebastian was initially a little hesitant, but after a while, we managed to convince him. We helped him sit on the red machine. The owner started the engine, then, under full control, began twisting the throttle up and down, resulting in a loud exhaust sound. The smell of exhaust fumes was in the air. The entire scooter rally lasted no longer than 20 minutes. It would be difficult for me to thank each person individually, and the sound of revving scooters made it impossible. So, I thanked the organizer for everything. I promised to count the contents of the envelope today and let him know how much was collected.

Everyone left, leaving behind a cloud of smoke.

Sitting on the couch in the evening after a day full of excitement, Eve and I opened the taped, transparent envelope. We took out the banknotes and laid the coins on the table. We counted everything carefully. We were surprised because we collected over 100 pounds in total! I immediately informed the organizers about the amount collected by sending a message with thanks.

The model of the machine that is still with us today

Together Again, Son

One father is more than a hundred schoolmasters.

George Herbert

Lying in bed in the morning, I stared at the ceiling. I couldn't stop thinking about why our life had unfolded this way. Many questions swirled in my head for which I had no answers. Why is Natalie's story such a big puzzle with no logical explanation? Why did Sebastian get sick? I could keep lying there and pondering, but it was high time to get up.

In a few days, Eve and Natalie were going to fly to Poland. They had to take care of certain matters and visit family they hadn't seen in a long time.

Natalie had never flown on a plane before. I was curious about how the child would handle the flight. Sebastian, at a similar age to his sister, simply slept through the plane journey. The flights from Leeds to Gdansk were always in the evening, so there was a good chance that the child would sleep during the trip. A few days before the departure, Natalie had another journey waiting for her. It was the hospital where she had previously been hospitalized, albeit a different ward. The reason for the visit was a procedure. She was supposed to have the gastrostomy tube removed, leaving a tiny button. Since the surgery, the child had a long, hanging tube for feeding. As Natalie grew, we decided to change that. Such a button would make it easier for her to function, especially since the little one was already crawling and the hanging tube was bothering her. She could climb the stairs on her own on all fours in our house. It was everywhere, so the procedure was simply necessary.

I didn't want my wife to go with her to the hospital. I said I would go and take care of it. I would be with her the whole time until she fell asleep. The child was going to be put under general anesthesia. Otherwise, the procedure would have been impossible.

When the day of the operation came, I put Natalie in the stroller, and we made our way to the station. This time, I tried to time it so that we would be there right on time before the train departed. I knew Natalie didn't like loud noises, so I wanted to spare her from the rushing express trains passing our railway station.

We arrived at the location. The entrance to the hospital was on the other side, different from the one we used with Sebastian. The area in front of the facility was very familiar to me. I noticed a bench nearby. It was the same bench where our whole family sat when Natalie could go outside the hospital walls for the first time. I looked at my daughter. She stared at the bench as if she remembered being there. After a moment, she raised her head and started looking at the crown of the same tree she saw for the first time outside the hospital walls a few years ago. She fell silent, gazing ahead, while the multicolored leaves fluttered in the light breeze. Everything looked just like it did back then. I didn't want to stay here any longer. This place stirred up mixed feelings in me. On one hand, happiness because we went outside with Natalie for the first time. On the other hand, sadness that we were in this place and fighting for our daughter's life.

I headed towards the entrance of the facility. In front of the doors, I saw people of various ages in hospital attire, smoking their cigarettes. Some of them were in wheelchairs, while others held intravenous poles with one hand. It's not for me to judge. I'm not a smoker, and it's hard for me to imagine how strong of an addiction it must be.

We entered the hospital. We took an elevator to the upper floor and proceeded to the reception area. After registration, we were instructed to sit and wait for the doctor to call us. The waiting room was filled with families. Some children ran around the room, while others sat at a small table coloring various pictures. I sat in a chair, and my fatigue was so great that my eyes kept closing as if I were nodding off. After a while, I heard my daughter's name being called. I got up, rubbing my eyes, picked up Natalie, and followed the doctor's assistant.

Natalie sat on a hospital bed, and I took a seat in the nearby chair. We were supposed to wait for the doctor.

About 30 minutes passed, and then a tall doctor in a white coat appeared. He greeted us and asked me to lay the child on her back and roll up her shirt. He placed his open hand near the gastrostomy site and began to gently press it in various places.

When he finished the initial examination, he took his hand away and turned his face towards me. He declared that there was something blocking where the gastrostomy is currently located. He added that he wouldn't be able to place a new button in the same spot.

I asked him if he was joking. In response, I heard that he wasn't. That they would simply close up the old site, and the button would be installed next to it. Another scar, right? I firmly stated that I needed to discuss this with my wife, but I guaranteed that Eve would not agree to it for sure. After so many experiences, I knew that every matter should be approached with caution. To weigh all the pros and cons and make a decision based on that. I took out my phone from my pocket and called Eve. I presented everything to her and only asked if I should go home. Both of us were in agreement that our child should not be operated on in a different place again!

After the conversation with my wife, I didn't even sit down. The doctor was waiting for my decision. I replied that he should examine her again. If something continued to block and hinder the procedure, I would take my daughter home. I reiterated that I disagreed with my wife on placing the button anywhere other than where the feeding tube is currently located, and during the consultation, it was explicitly stated that the change would occur in the same spot.

The doctor sighed but examined her once more. He pressed with his hand again, this time a bit harder. At some point, he smiled. I looked at him, waiting for an answer. He said that Natalie was ready for the procedure, that there was no longer any blockage, and they would be able to insert the feeding button in the same place.

I called Eve again. I explained the situation once more. This time, we agreed.

Together with my daughter and the doctors, we took the elevator down to the room where the procedure was to take place. General anesthesia was necessary, so I stayed with Natalie until she fell asleep. I gave her a kiss on the cheek, closed the door behind me, and headed to the hospital cafeteria. I was already very hungry. I had no idea how long all of this would take.

After I had eaten, I returned to the room. I waited for them to bring my daughter back. After a while, I lost track of time. I stopped looking at the clock. I couldn't even doze off because there was a crying baby in the room next door.

When they brought Natalie back to the room, the baby was still asleep. I was told that she should wake up soon. The procedure went as planned. Now they need to observe how our daughter feels after the anesthesia. If everything is fine, we should be discharged in less than 2 hours.

I informed Eve that everything went well, and we're waiting for the discharge. I also mentioned that I didn't know what time I would be home and advised her not to wait for me with dinner.

The entire hospital stay took place on May 17, three days before my girls' flight to Poland.

When I got back home, it was already dark outside. I quickly told Eve about the whole incident. She just shook her head from side to side, not believing that they wanted our child to have another scar.

I helped Eve dress the little one in her pajamas, and we put her to sleep. I checked on Sebastian; he was sleeping. I gave him a kiss and then went to the bathroom to take a hot bath. It was a moment of relaxation for me after a tough day.

May 20 came. The day when Sebastian and I took Eve and Natalie to the airport. We helped carry all the luggage, then went to the counter, waiting for special assistance. I kissed and hugged the girls goodbye. Sebastian and I wished them a safe flight.

We returned to the car that we had left in the free parking lot. Closing the door, I said to Sebastian that we were together again, just like a couple of years ago when I flew with him to Poland. I promised him that we would make the most of our time together.

I turned the key in the ignition. Gently releasing the clutch, we set off on the road back home.

My daughter and I in the hospital while waiting for the procedure

Supercar Festival

*In order to succeed, your desire for success should be greater than
your fear of failure.*

Bill Cosby

It was a very strange feeling lying alone in bed in the morning. I was
certain that my girls were well taken care of in Poland. They deserved
this trip so much. Eve hadn't been back to her family home since Natalie was born. She missed her family so much that as soon as the opportunity arose, we bought cheap plane tickets.

They were supposed to return home on June 8, a day before Natalie's third birthday.

Sebastian was still asleep. While sipping my coffee, I glanced at
the large A4 sheet attached to the fridge with magnets. I double-checked the entire medication schedule. Whenever my son received a particular medicine, I would immediately mark it with a circle on the sheet
to ensure no doses were missed or, worse, given twice! I used a pen or
a black marker for this crucial task. The schedule was laid out for the
entire week. At each hospital visit, I would receive a new sheet and a
bag full of medications from the hospital pharmacy.

With such responsibility, I double-checked everything. Did the dosage match? Were the syringes disposed of in the designated container?
Did I have a supply of sugar-free juices to mix with the medicine? The
list of duties was quite extensive.

I sat down in a chair, took my phone in hand, and checked the fundraisers I had initiated. I thanked everyone from the bottom of my he-

art, leaving a comment on each post.

My medical leave limit was approaching its end in early August. Time was running out. I still hadn't received any response from the authorities regarding Sebastian's disability allowance. The person who helped us fill out all the paperwork assured us not to worry. She said that if a child had cancer, the authorities would automatically assign them the highest disability group. The only downside was the excruciatingly long wait for the decision letter.

In the meantime, my wife and I applied for a benefit called Universal Credit. It was our last resort. I knew I wouldn't be physically able to go to work. With two children who required so much care, I was needed at home. I don't even want to imagine how tough it would be for my wife if she were alone with the kids for over 8 hours.

We searched for solutions in many ways. We never expected that we would have to rely on benefits. We didn't want to use them, but we had no choice.

After breakfast, I drove Sebastian to school. I gave him a high-five and a fist bump, wishing him a great day.

I returned home, turned on the computer, and continued writing my book. The first chapters were taking shape. I had all the events chronologically recorded in a notebook. I truly believed that if the book succeeded in the market, I would be able to break free from the shackles of the benefits I had to receive.

Time passed quickly as I wrote. Before I knew it, it was time to pick up Sebastian.

In the afternoon, we were supposed to call my wife, Eve. He took my phone and opened the app we were meant to use to connect. He came running to me full of energy. Gently hopping and pulling on my pants, he desperately wanted me to look at the phone. There was an advertisement for an event that was supposed to take place the following Saturday – a supercar festival. The child tugging at my pant leg really wanted us to go there.

I had mixed feelings. On the one hand, I had to keep a tight rein on all expenses. On the other hand, Sebastian had been through so much in the past months that I wanted to somehow compensate him – to let him forget about hospitals, medications, trains, and so on, even if only for one day. I stroked his head, confirming that we would go to the festival. My son started jumping with joy, thanking me and hugging me tightly.

We called Eve. From what she told me, the weather in Poland was very nice. My wife was resting, and Natalie was crawling around the living room, moving dark green-leafed plants in a pot. She was curious about the world. We didn't have any potted plants on the floor at our home, so she was even more intrigued by the white pots. I chatted with Eve for a while, then hung up, wishing everyone a great day. I returned to the living room. Sebastian had put on a TV show about fast cars. He wanted me to sit beside him and watch it together. When I saw the smile on his face, my heart rejoiced. I decided that I would order the tickets online in the evening when I had more time. I also wanted to calmly read the description of the entire festival.

I spent the next hours with Sebastian, playing with him in his room. Ever since he heard we were going, he had only taken out the sports cars from the large box. We played, arranging them in various rows and racing them on the track made from blocks.

Evening came. Outside, the moon was full, and the stars shone in the sky.

I turned on the computer. First, I wrote to Eve, telling her how our day went. Then I clicked on the link to the festival's website. I read every detail about the event. Next, I opened the "Buy Tickets" tab. No, this can't be happening! I had promised my son we would go, and all the tickets were already sold out! I started wondering what to do next. The only right solution was to write an email to the organizer, asking if we could still buy tickets at the entrance to the festival. I added that my son really wanted to be there.

It didn't even take 10 minutes from sending the message when I received a reply via email. It said that it was perfectly fine to buy tickets on the spot. If there were any issues, please print this email and show it at the ticket booth.

I felt relieved. I would have felt really foolish if I had let him down. I printed the email. I wanted to have it ready. Then I opened my writing software and wrote a few pages of the book. That would be enough for today. I shut down the computer, went downstairs, and watched some television. I needed to relax a bit after the whole day.

The next days passed quickly for us. On Thursday, we had chemotherapy. I made sure that my son received his medication every day. It was a very tough job. I had to remember everything. The most crucial thing was not to make any mistakes with the doses. I also had to keep an eye on whether the child had a fever, vomiting, or diarrhea. Any of my concerns had to be reported to the clinic immediately. If necessary, we had to go for a check-up, even in the middle of the night. I also made sure that the car was always fully fueled. Any mishaps were out of the question.

When I woke up in the morning, Sebastian was already awake. He was very happy because the day he had been waiting for so long had finally come - the day of the supercar festival.

It turned out that an acquaintance was also going, so early in the morning, we set off together in one car.

Arriving at the venue, you could feel the opulence. Hundreds of supercars were parked on a vast green area. Walking among the cars, I learned that there was also an opportunity to talk to the owners of these beautiful machines. I was most interested in what these people did for a living to afford such marvels. Literally, everything was there, from classic Lamborghini Diablos to Bugatti Veyrons. Right next to it was a racetrack where they showcased the accelerations of certain models. Thousands of people came to this festival. Sebastian had a lot of joy on the entire trip. So did I. I went there for inspiration. Such an event motivated me to continue my personal development. I made a promise to myself. Someday, I'll go to such a festival with my supercar, along with Sebastian, to showcase my car. Of course, I couldn't afford it at that time. I decided to make every effort to achieve financial success in the future.

The sound from the car exhausts was sometimes too loud for my son. It happened that when we were walking among the cars, some of them had their engines running, and the owners showcased the noise by pressing the gas pedal. In those moments, Sebastian covered his ears but continued to admire how beautiful the world of cars could be. The event was still ongoing, but we decided to head back home. We had been there for a few hours, and you could see that the child was getting tired.

Upon returning home, Sebastian called his mom. He excitedly told her everything.

His smile never left his face.

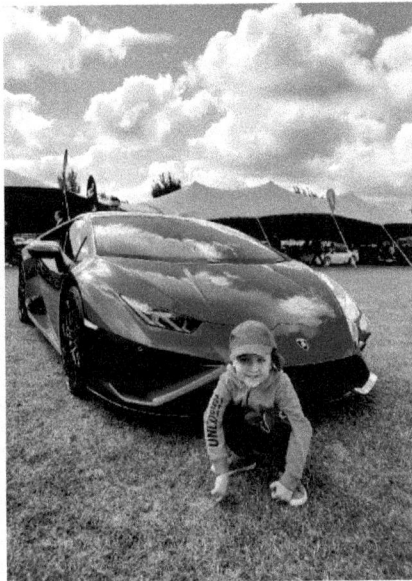

Supercar Festival

Is it a coincidence?

Throughout life, respect the truth so that your words are more credible than the promises of others.

Socrates

It was June 8th. Sebastian and I were waiting at the airport for Eve and Natalie. I held a bouquet of tea roses - Eve's favorite color. Sebastian, on the other hand, held a chocolate plaque that he wanted to give to his mom. Natalie could have a taste too, even though she had a gastrostomy, the doctors allowed the child to receive a small amount of food in her mouth.

People started coming out through the gates, but we couldn't see our girls. We waited a bit longer. Suddenly, we spotted our family. Sebastian quickly ran to his mom and hugged her with all his strength, not even allowing her to put her suitcase aside. He said he missed his mom and sister a lot and was very happy they were back. After a moment, he greeted Natalie and gave her a piece of chocolate. I approached my wife, handing her the bouquet of roses. I hugged her gently. I kissed her. I also had a small gift for our daughter, even though it was modest. Just like Sebastian, she liked to play with toy cars. While at the festival, as souvenirs, I bought Sebastian and Natalie each a little toy car. She was so delighted with the gift that she began to slowly unwrap the packaging.

I took the heavy suitcase from Eve. It weighed about 20 kg. We went to the car. When everyone was comfortably seated, we headed back home on the highway. Natalie was very cheerful. The next day, she was going to celebrate her 3rd birthday! I was very happy that the whole family was together again.

The sound of the alarm woke me up in the morning. I was sleep-deprived. I yawned, rubbed my eyes, and put on my glasses. Slightly drowsy, I went to the kitchen. I poured coffee into a glass, waiting for the water to boil. It was my habit. I started every day with black coffee without milk and sugar.

I sat at the table. I unlocked my phone and started replying to all those who had supported us in the fundraisers. I kept wondering how long we would have to wait for a response from the authorities?

To have the strength for the whole day, I prepared a bacon and egg scramble for myself and Eve. However, the children wanted omelets with raspberry jam.

During breakfast, the first phone call with birthday wishes for Natalie came from my mom. Then the phones rang periodically.

We had a custom of giving the birthday present only after blowing out the candles. So Natalie had to wait a few more hours. The day passed, and we cherished every moment.

Sipping green tea, I heard the mail carrier sliding letters through the door. There were a few of them. I began to go through all the envelopes. To my eyes, the one we had been waiting for so long was there! I sat in the kitchen for a moment, then gently opened the envelope's contents. I smiled. Sebastian was granted the highest-level allowance until 2025! I was very happy because it was supposed to make things much easier for us during the long period of treatment! Hospital trips would no longer be such a financial burden as they had been so far.

I set the letter aside and checked the next one. Apart from a water bill, there was another envelope - from a foundation. After reading the contents, I became even happier! It said that the foundation was sending us for a four-day holiday on August 12th, which would take place in a cottage by the sea in Wales, near the town of Tenby!

I was surprised. Two such wonderful letters received in one day. I shared the information with Eve, who was dressing up Natalie in a beautiful dress - a pattern of pink flowers intertwined with multicolored leaves, perfectly suited for our daughter.

We didn't invite guests. We wanted to spend this time with our closest family. We didn't have the strength to organize a big birthday party.

We stuck three candles into a piece of store-bought cheesecake and lit them. Everyone sang the birthday song for Natalie. We were happy! After a moment, we told Natalie to make a wish and then blow out the candles. She took a deep breath and blew out the three candles with all her might.

Right after she did that, the phone rang. The number was unknown, but I answered it. I asked how I could help?

They were calling from oncology. They wanted to discuss with me Sebastian's latest blood test results.

Worry overcame me. I felt a slight stress. My fingers began to sweat, and I felt a slight tremor. I never liked such situations. I swallowed and asked them to continue.

Over the phone, I heard that the blood tests clearly indicated that cancer had been defeated, and Sebastian was moving on to the maintenance stage until 2025.

I was speechless. I didn't know what to say. I just looked at Natalie, and she smiled at me. It was as if she wanted to convey something to me. Did she think of this while blowing out the candles? That her brother would recover? Was that her birthday wish?

The voice on the phone interrupted my mental journey. I thanked them for the information and wished them a good day.

My concerned wife, seeing my expression, approached me. She asked why I was so surprised. Who called, and what did they want? I hugged her. I told her that the clinic had called .Over the phone, I heard that the blood tests clearly indicated that cancer had been defeated, and Sebastian was moving on to the maintenance stage until 2025. Now we only had the long road ahead to complete the maintenance.

Was it a coincidence that the cancer disappeared on Natalie's birthday? I don't think so.

When the children had already gone to sleep, Eve and I sat on the couch in the living room. We wanted to take a moment to relax after the exhausting but happy day. We started watching a Viking series, which interested us the most.

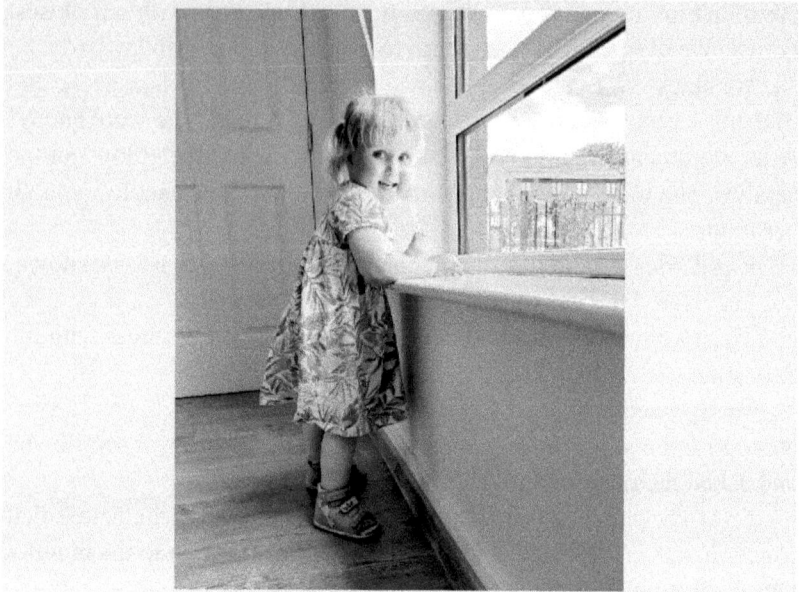

Natalie on her birthday

True Warrior

I can accept failure, everyone fails at something. But I can't accept not trying.

Michael Jordan

Although the cancer was gone, the intense treatment for my son wasn't supposed to end until the end of July. Until then, we had to go for chemotherapy every Thursday.

Sebastian, despite the medication he was taking, tried to be an active child. He loved sports, not just running, but also soccer. His favorite was always obstacle course races. He had participated in a few of them before, and it was evident he wanted to take part again.

The port, which was implanted under his skin, posed a challenge for him on the obstacle course. It was small, but that was the spot where our son had a needle inserted every week to draw blood and receive medication in the clinic. At the end of each oncology visit, they would remove the needle and apply a small plaster.

When the port was implanted, the doctors told us to be careful. If it shifted accidentally, it would need to be repositioned. We wanted to avoid this scenario, as Sebastian would have to undergo general anesthesia, something he was terribly afraid of.

During his treatment, there were times when he needed a lumbar puncture. To receive the injection, he had to undergo general anesthesia. Many times, the day before the procedure, he felt unwell. His stomach hurt, and his hands trembled.

If only I could take on all his suffering. All I could do was to be with him all the time and provide support.

At the end of June, there were obstacle course races for kids called 'Junior Warrior.' They were located nearby, in Leeds. One day, our son asked if he could participate. He really wanted to return to the starting line. I told him that I understood, but we needed to discuss it with the doctor. I explained to him that he had a port, and any movement of it would require a hospital visit. I also added that we didn't know how long we would stay there.

He had a sad expression. He started to get angry with me. I hugged him. I knew that his demeanor was influenced by the medication. I was aware that I couldn't agree to everything. Offended, he went to his room, stomping loudly on the stairs. As he headed to his room, he shouted that it was unfair. He didn't cry, but he slammed the door to his room and lay down in his bed, falling asleep.

I wondered whether to call the clinic. Sebastian was being aggressive. If I felt something troubling, I was supposed to contact them.

Eve suggested I wait because he had gone to sleep, and we would see what mood he would be in when he woke up.

The ticket prices for the obstacle course races for kids were not expensive. It was a cost I could afford. I had to wait to make a decision until Thursday - for the consultation with the oncologist.

Hours passed, and Sebastian was still sleeping. He woke up maybe after 4 hours. He came up to me, hugged me, and said, 'Good morning, Dad.'

It looked as if he didn't remember the whole incident at all. After a while, he asked if I could cook him some pasta and fry 2 eggs.

It's amazing how the human brain works. He didn't remember the whole incident at all.

When Sebastian was diagnosed with the disease, I already had a ticket for the Ultra Warrior race. I always wanted to try a long-distance race. The competition was supposed to take place on Sunday, June 26. There was one problem. I wasn't prepared for this race at all, and I couldn't sell the ticket to someone else. I also knew that if I went alone, Sebastian would be very disappointed. Unfortunately, we had to wait for the decision whether he could go with me. I preferred to know the oncologist's opinion. My subconscious told me that he would probably be against it.

During Sebastian's intensive treatment, we had three very long clinic visits. We already had two of them. The third one was supposed to be the longest. It was estimated that the therapy would take over 4 hours. This therapy was scheduled for this week. Then there would be weekly visits to the clinic until the end of this cycle.

We were told that after 6 months of intensive treatment, hospital visits would become less frequent.

The next day, our whole family went for a walk. We were enjoying the beautiful weather. We had a huge park behind our house. It was created on the grounds of an old mine. There were plenty of walking paths, and Sebastian and Natalie loved the ones that led uphill. They enjoyed looking at the view of our town from the park's highest peak. All around, you could see beautiful plants. There was also a pond where we often spotted swans and ducks. We loved taking walks in that place. It was always a moment of relaxation for us.

As for the upcoming race, which was supposed to last for 5 hours, I was rather indifferent. I wasn't prepared, and I didn't follow any specific diet. My training was sporadic at best. I told myself that if I couldn't make it, I would simply drop out of the race. I didn't have the opportunity to prepare properly for this run.

It was getting late, and the sun started to set, changing the color of the sky to orange.

Refreshed by the fresh air, we returned home, and the children fell asleep quickly in the evening.

It was Thursday - the day we were supposed to spend in the clinic. Eve helped me pack a backpack with food. It was quite heavy. I didn't expect that provisions could weigh so much.

Sebastian said goodbye to his mom and Natalie. We headed towards the train station on foot. We left the car with Eve so she could take Natalie to kindergarten.

Upon arriving at the clinic, we sat in the hospital waiting room. After the routine check of measuring and weighing, we went to the room. There was a bed waiting for Sebastian there. I had a blue chair with wooden armrests nearby. Two nurses set up a stand with a large syringe filled with red liquid. They connected the cable to the port that was sewn under my son's skin. They set the machine for over 4 hours, and the medication was flowing slowly.

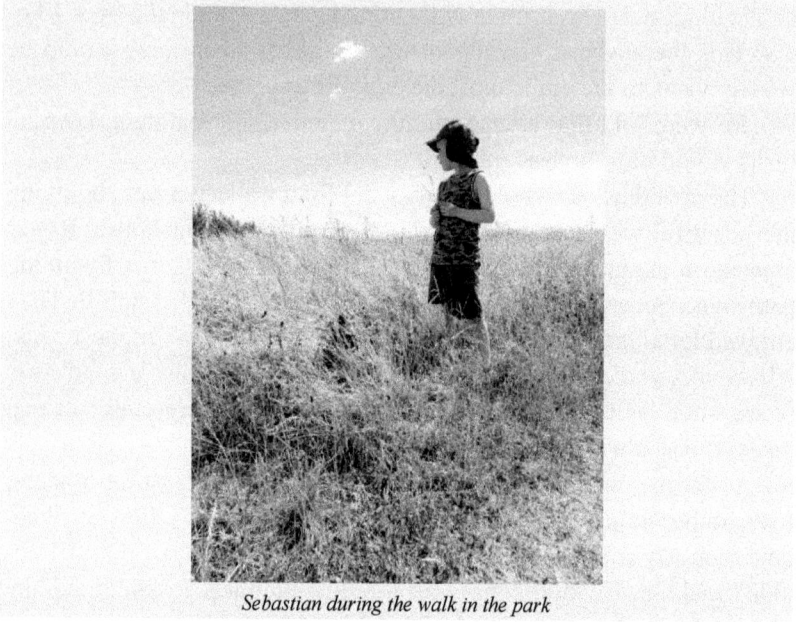

Sebastian during the walk in the park

Sebastian took his tablet out of the backpack. I helped him connect to the hospital's internet. Once we had access, Sebastian set up his favorite cartoon about the adventures of a yellow sponge.

I asked the nurse if she could call the oncologist. I wanted to talk to him about the race. In response, I was told that they would pass on the information, and if the doctor had a moment, he would come to me.

Time was passing slowly. Every now and then, I glanced at the machine, looking at its display. Sebastian fell asleep. Sitting in the chair, I connected to the hospital's internet on my phone. I replied with thanks to all the people who supported us. Then I opened a notepad and started writing another chapter of the book. I didn't want to waste this time on nonsense like watching TV shows or playing games. Time was running out. I had to give a final answer at work by August 10 - whether I was returning or not. I still didn't have any response from the authorities regarding benefits. Looking at the situation, I couldn't go back to work. I thought that writing the book would help me as an additional source of income.

I was writing on my phone, and my work was interrupted by the oncologist who came. I saved the file, then told him about the race. I added that the child had gone through a lot, and I thought such a diversion would do him good. He could forget about the place he was currently in, at least for a moment.

The doctor sighed. He said that I was right to some extent. However, he was concerned that the port might be damaged. He added that he couldn't make the decision for me. If I decided to let my son participate, I would have to watch over him very closely.

After that conversation, the oncologist handed me the results of my son's blood tests. Then he gave me a form for another appointment. I had to take the printed piece of paper to the reception every time I did this, I'd hurriedly grab a free ticket for the oncology parking. Sometimes the trains weren't running. In those cases, the only mode of transport was coming by car.

Sebastian woke up and asked if I had talked to the doctor. I replied that I did. I told him we would go to the race, but on the condition that he would stay close to me. If he couldn't overcome an obstacle or if it would jeopardize the port, we would leave it behind.

With the cable connected to his body, Sebastian threw himself into my arms and hugged me tightly. He thanked me. I knew that this was all I could do for him.

The treatment came to an end. We received a mesh bag full of medications and another dosage schedule. When we returned home, it was already dark outside.

I sat down with my son at the computer. We ordered a ticket for the obstacle race for him. Once again, a smile appeared on the face of the little warrior.

A week had passed since we bought the ticket. Saturday, the day of the departure, had arrived. We packed everything we needed: shoes, shirts, drinks, socks, and so on... The backpack was bursting at the seams. I barely managed to zip it up. I loaded everything into the trunk, then we hit the road with the whole family.

The entire sports village was on the outskirts of Leeds. We went to registration, collected our starter kit, and then returned to the car to change. Sebastian was incredibly excited to have the opportunity to stand on the starting line again.

The countdown began. When we heard the signal, we set off on the 3-kilometer course full of obstacles, mud, and water. We didn't rush. Our goal was to cross the finish line. We tackled all the obstacles with caution. I was very careful not to damage the port. When we reached the finish line, Eve and Natalie were lying on a blanket not far away. Sebastian started shouting towards them to get their attention. They waved at us with smiles.

We did it! We made it again! We crossed the finish line! Sebastian proved once again that he is a true warrior. He also proved that limitations exist only in our minds.

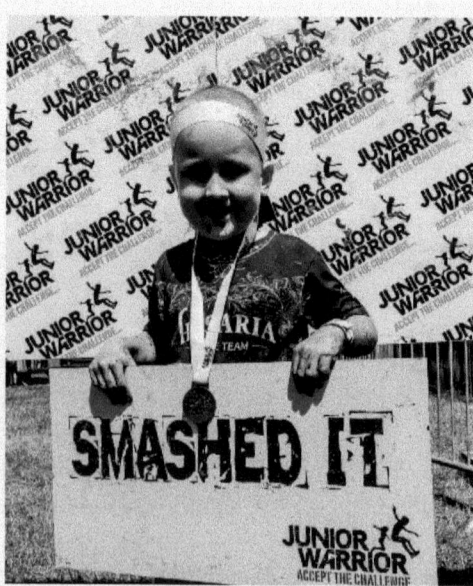

A true warrior

I got emotional. A tear welled up in my eye. Every day, he showed how strong he was and fought for a better tomorrow. Just like his sister, whose story I described in my first book.

At the finish line, a few commemorative photos were taken by a professional photographer.

After a short photo session, we headed towards where our family was resting. Eve and Natalie sat on a green blanket with white flowers. Next to them lay an open backpack containing clean clothes for Sebastian. I had left mine in the car, so I asked Eve for the keys. I fastened the backpack and called my son to go with me.

After such runs, we always put our dirty clothes and shoes in a trash bag. It was one of the simplest ways to avoid getting the car dirty with mud. We changed, then went back for Eve and Natalie, inviting them for ice cream and pizza.

There was always plenty of food to choose from in the village. We split into two lines. Eve and the kids were after ice cream, and I was in line for pizza. Well-fed, we returned home. Tomorrow, a grueling run awaited me.

The alarm clock rang at 5 in the morning. I got up and double-checked if I had packed everything. While everyone was still asleep, I set out on the journey.

Upon arrival, I picked up my race kit. I put a red band on my head. I attached my race number to my shorts with four tiny silver safety pins. I positioned myself at the starting line. I told myself that whatever would be, would be. The countdown finished, and I started forward.

I was just 2 kilometers away from completing three full laps. I was very satisfied with myself. Despite the lack of preparation, I managed to cover a distance of over 30 kilometers!

I received my dream medal. Then, with a slow pace, I headed back to the village to replenish the lost carbohydrates. I ordered two pizzas. As I sat down, my body was so exhausted that I had to find a point of support.

Tired, I returned home. This weekend was really successful. We could all take a break from the hospital, if only for a moment. We spent quality time together.

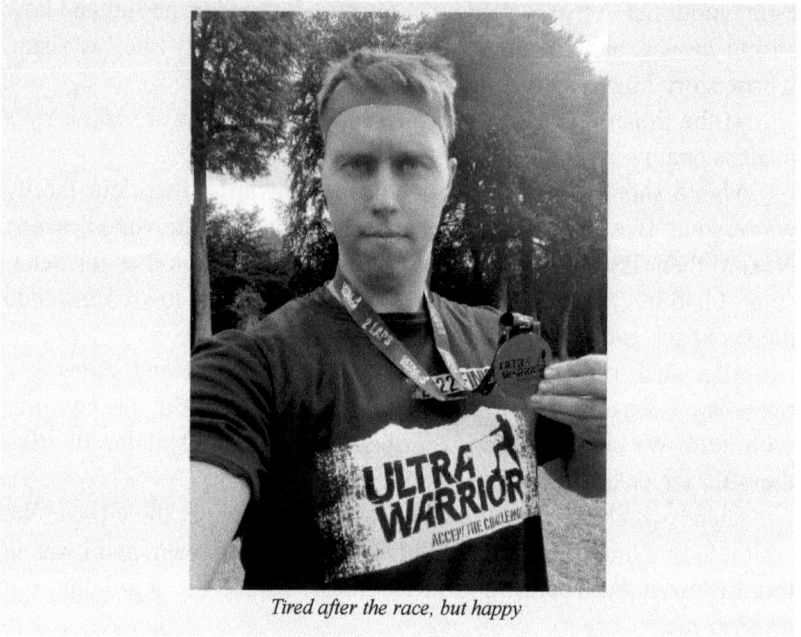

Tired after the race, but happy

Cottage, tranquility, and the sound of the sea

It's lack of faith that makes people afraid of meeting challenges, and I believed in myself.

Muhammad Ali

Since our last races, almost a month has passed. In the meantime, Sebastian completed the intensive treatment cycle. From that moment on, our hospital visits were supposed to become less frequent week by week. We had been visiting the clinic regularly every Thursday. During that time, our son didn't experience any unpleasant incidents that would require an extra hospital visit.

One day, I received a letter from work. I had to make the final decision on whether I was returning or not. I arranged a meeting and handed in the letter requesting a one-year career break.

With my basic allowances secured, I could comfortably afford this maneuver. Everything was falling into place. While the treatment period was very long, now I was needed at home more than ever, and I didn't have the physical capability to return to work.

One of my social media fundraisers had concluded. Sitting at the computer, I took a break from writing the book and opened my profile. I wrote a post in which I expressed heartfelt gratitude to everyone for their kindness and support for our family. I thanked them for providing us with courage and motivation to fight the illness. I was sure that without all of them, I wouldn't have made it.

The second fundraiser was still open, but we didn't share it publicly anymore. The only reason for keeping it open was related to waiting for a transfer from the school. The funds collected during the school's masquerade ball were supposed to be transferred there. For some reason, this didn't happen. Several months had passed since that event, so we contacted the school. Although we didn't like to remind them, we had no other choice. The lady at the reception said they would get in touch with the foundation and keep us informed. We thanked her.

In the kitchen, next to the fridge, hung a calendar. Our schedule was very tight, so we had all the dates and times of appointments written there. In addition to Sebastian's hospital visits, Natalie also had many appointments.

Orthopedists, kidney, liver, and bladder ultrasounds, physiotherapists - that's just the beginning of a long list. We tried to organize all the visits so that we could have them behind us before going on vacation. Thanks to the foundation, we had the opportunity to go to the seaside in Wales for four days.

Some dates didn't work for us, so we rescheduled a few appointments to a later date. Another Thursday visit to oncology was still ahead of us.

I pulled dusty suitcases out of the closet, cleaned them, and then helped Eve with packing. My assistance lasted for less than an hour. Later, I had to meet up with Sebastian to catch a train; we had an appointment at the clinic. We all couldn't wait for the trip; we had been waiting for it for so long.

Early on Friday, we planned to hit the road, which was supposed to take over 7 hours. Counting all the stops along the way, we estimated that the journey might even extend to 10 hours. I was sure that two kids wouldn't endure such a long time in the car, and we would have to take breaks, alternating diaper changes and meal breaks.

The departure day arrived. We got up early. I loaded the stroller, two suitcases, and four backpacks into the car. We had breakfast, and then we put the kids in the car. When everyone was ready to leave, I double-checked everything. Gas off, lights off, garden door locked, windows closed. Everything was in order. When I was a teenager, I once left the stove on for half a day. Luckily, it was electric, and there were no dishes on the burner. Since then, I check everything meticulously a few times. I locked the door, turned the key in the ignition, and we set off on the long-awaited vacation.

As we drove through beautiful landscapes, stood in unwanted traffic jams, after nearly 10 hours, we reached our destination. We collected the keys to the cottage, unpacked all our luggage, and then looked around. I stretched my bones, taking in a deep breath of fresh air.

Once we had familiarized ourselves with every room, we went out to the terrace.

Holidays in Wales thanks to the foundation

The view was stunning. In the background, you could see small cliffs and a little island.

The kids fell asleep quickly after the long journey. Eve and I sat on the terrace, listening to the sound of the sea. We raised a toast with a glass of wine to celebrate that everything was slowly falling into place. Now, we were enjoying a moment of peace away from our daily routine.

Our trip only lasted for 4 days, two of which we had to dedicate to travel to and from the destination. When Saturday came, we headed to the nearby town of Tenby.

It was the holiday season, and there were so many tourists that finding a parking spot was a challenge. We didn't have parking permits for disabled spaces at that time. Eve and the kids got out of the car and sat on a bench on the other side of the street. I searched for an available spot and managed to park on the top floor after 20 minutes.

Navigating through narrow, tiny streets towards the beach, we squeezed our way through the crowds of tourists. It was really crowded. We reached our destination. The kids played in the sand. Despite the bright sun in the sky, the sea water was too cold to swim in.

We spent about 3 hours on the beach. We got hungry, and Eve had prepared a list of places where we could eat well. She selected them based on online reviews. We headed to the first place, but seeing the long line, we gave up and went to the second. There, the line was shorter, so we decided to stay.

The restaurant had a very cozy atmosphere, reflecting coastal vibes in its interior design. We ordered fries with ketchup, a piece of chicken, and a salad for the kids. As for us, we had mussels in garlic sauce, steak with cheese, and vegetables. The food was delicious. We finished everything, and for dessert, my wife and I had a cup of coffee, and everyone had a small cake.

We weren't in a hurry anywhere. No deadlines were chasing us, no train schedules, and most importantly, no hospitals. Savouring our coffee, we cherished the moment.

The town was very beautiful. In contrast to other similar coastal towns, it stood out due to one view. All the houses by the sea were painted in enchanting colors, from blue to pink. The color palette was vast, with each building having a different hue.

It all looked so beautiful, like a pastel-painted picture. No wonder this place attracted such a large number of tourists.

As we walked through the narrow streets, we bought a souvenir fridge magnet. The next day, we planned to go to another beach in the same town. We returned to the resort after a very successful day. The rest of the day was spent the same way as yesterday - relaxing on the terrace and gazing at the sea.

The next day, I got up early, prepared breakfast for everyone. This time, we planned the trip more quickly.

We found a parking spot at the beach. If we had arrived 30 minutes later, everything would have already been taken.

In our opinion, this beach was more beautiful than the previous one. We relaxed, and the kids played in the sand. We had no other plans for that day. We spent the whole day at the beach, savoring the moment.

When we returned to the cottage, we started packing. It was a very successful and much-needed trip. I went to bed early. I had about 10 hours of the return journey ahead of me.

When I woke up in the morning, I was hit by a stomach flu. At that point, I knew that the journey back home would be very exhausting.

When it's too beautiful

There are plenty of difficult obstacles in your path. Don't allow yourself to become one of them.

Ralph Marston

The holidays passed quickly for us. September arrived. Natalie returned to preschool, and Sebastian to kindergarten. We had variable weather. One day the sun was shining, and the next day it rained. That's the charm of this country. You never know how to dress. Today, the weather happened to be moderate. There were clouds in the sky. A gentle breeze was blowing, and the temperature was at 25 degrees.

We dressed the children in their school uniforms. We got into the car and headed to the start of the school year.

Eve was taking Natalie to a different facility. In the one our son attended, the preschool didn't have an accessible bathroom for disabled individuals. We would only be able to change schools for Natalie when she enters reception. It was inconvenient and time-consuming for us, but we had no other choice.

The kids went to their classes. Eve and I returned home and started preparing lunch.

As Sebastian's oncology appointment approached, a nurse came to our home a few days earlier. She drew blood for tests and left the needle in the port through which our child received chemotherapy. This visit saved us time at the hospital. It was a significant convenience for me. By establishing this system, I saved a few hours. I could bring my son to the hospital only for measurements and weighing, and we didn't have to deal with blood draws and needle insertions.

This appointment was scheduled for the next morning, before Sebastian had to go to school.

We went to pick up Sebastian from his lessons. Natalie was home earlier because her classes only lasted for 3 hours. We had lunch and went for a walk to the park. The first day of school went very well for us.

The next day, I woke up earlier. I had my alarm set for 5 o'clock. I got up so early for one reason only. I wanted to continue writing my book before everyone else woke up. That was when I could focus the most on creating my work. I also wrote it in the evenings. I won't deny that there were moments during the writing when my tears fell onto the keyboard. Emotions were unavoidable. However, I knew that this book had to be written. It could later help other parents in difficult times.

The nurse was supposed to come around 7 in the morning. During the needle insertion procedure, Sebastian didn't cry. He sat quietly on the couch, watching his favorite cartoons. Everything took just under 5 minutes. At the end, the nurse asked me if our son was going for general anesthesia that Thursday. I answered, 'Yes.' He was starting a new cycle of treatment. Suddenly, Sebastian interrupted our conversation. Grabbing my shirt around my waist, he asked if he was going to sleep during the tests. When he heard that he was, he looked worried. He lowered his head but didn't say anything. At that time, I didn't realize what a grave mistake we made by saying that out loud.

Sebastian went to school, but I noticed something was off in his behavior. He wouldn't speak, wouldn't smile. The only thing he did was hold my hand on the way to school. When I asked him what was wrong, he replied, 'Nothing.'

The school bell rang, and the children lined up. I gave him a high-five goodbye and returned home.

I told my wife about our son's strange behavior. She replied that sometimes he's like that. One day he's cheerful and joyful, and the next day he can wreak havoc in the house. We explained it by assuming that it was probably a side effect of the medication he had to take.

Around halfway through his lessons, the phone rang. It was the school calling to pick up our son earlier because he wasn't feeling well. He complained about a stomachache.

I got in the car and brought him home.

He didn't want to eat anything. He didn't even change and went straight to bed. Eve measured his temperature. It was normal. We let him rest and kept a close eye on his behavior.

Sebastian woke up after about 3 hours. He came downstairs, but he had a sad expression all the time, as if he were scared of something. Every time we tried to talk to him, he replied that nothing was wrong, just that he was tired.

The next day, we decided not to send him to school. We wanted him to rest before the hospital visit.

Evening came. We put Natalie to bed. I went downstairs to do the dishes, and Eve stayed in our son's room. She noticed that he had started to sweat. He was sleeping restlessly. However, his temperature wasn't elevated.

We went to bed. I was in for a long day ahead.

While I was sleeping, I felt a strong tug on my shoulder and some whispering. I woke up. It was 2 in the morning. Eve told me to get dressed and quickly take Sebastian to oncology. His temperature had crossed 38 degrees. This meant we had to head to the clinic immediately.

I splashed my face with cold water to wake up. I packed a bag in the car and set the navigation. Meanwhile, Eve changed our son out of his sweaty clothes. He could barely make it to the car. As I was leaving, Eve informed the clinic that we were on our way.

I had over 40 minutes of driving ahead of me. I sped up wherever I could. The motorway in Leeds was under construction all the time. Speed limits of 40 miles per hour didn't help me at all. If it weren't for the speed cameras standing next to them, I probably would have exceeded the limit several times.

I reached the destination.

We were supposed to go to the first floor. The clinic on floor C was only opening in the morning. I rang the bell. They admitted us, then showed us a bed. Sebastian lay down and fell asleep. I asked the nurse for a vomit bowl. The child complained of a stomachache, so anything was possible.

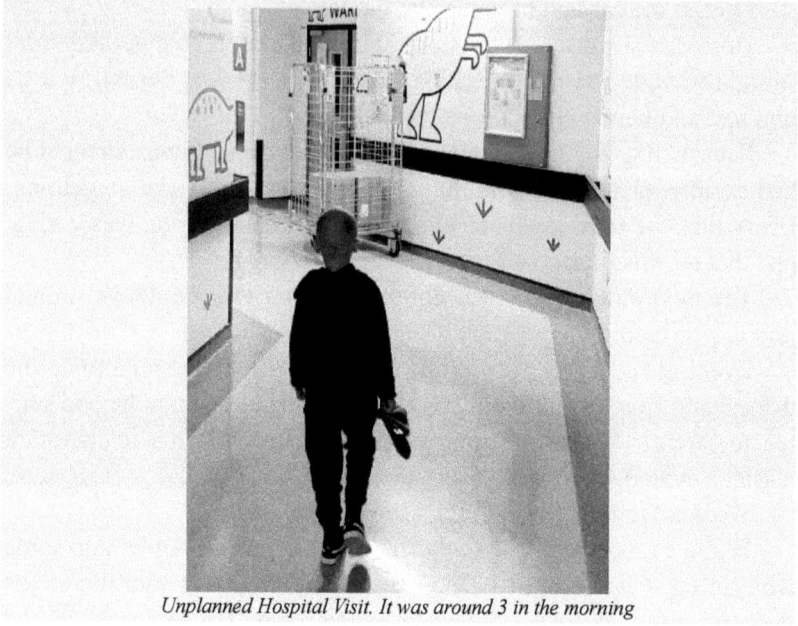

Unplanned Hospital Visit. It was around 3 in the morning

All the basic tests were done. I reclined on a fold-out chair next to my son, holding his hand. That's how we spent the night. When morning came, the clinic on floor C had received all the necessary information. My son's temperature had dropped. We just had to wait for someone from oncology to come for us.

Sebastian was completely stressed. He just kept looking at the door to see if anyone was coming. This moment didn't last long. The doctor came and said we could go upstairs now. Before entering the elevator, Sebastian grabbed onto me tightly and didn't want to go. He cried. Tears welled up in my eyes too, seeing his suffering. But I couldn't do anything. We entered the room where the anesthesiologists were waiting for us. The child flailed his arms and legs, kicking one of the doctors. He fell asleep after receiving the white fluid through the port. After this incident, I decided that it couldn't continue like this. I wanted to talk to the oncologist about the situation.

I waited in the waiting room until my son woke up. Then they were supposed to call me and show me the bed where Sebastian was lying.

I kept sending all the updates to my wife. She was worried about us.

While writing another message to Eve, I was called by a nurse. I went to my son, and he was hugging his favorite stuffed animal. It was Goofy, which he received from my mom as a gift a couple of years ago.

He woke up. He sat up and started looking around. When he saw me, he asked if he had been good? If he didn't cry? If I was proud of him? He didn't remember anything. For some reason, he was terribly afraid of this cycle of treatment. I gave him food and water. He was probably thirsty and hungry by then. He couldn't eat anything since yesterday's dinner before the general anesthesia.

While Sebastian was eating, the oncologist arrived. I told him that we needed to talk. I explained the whole situation to him. I asked him to have the anesthesiologist prescribe some calming medication for the next cycle. I couldn't allow my son to go through such stress again.

The doctor took notes of everything and then went on with his work.

The nurses observed Sebastian for another hour. When all the results had been checked, we were discharged.

We left the hospital after 11 hours. We returned home. After greeting his mom and sister, Sebastian went to play on the console.

I sat down with Eve in the kitchen. Together we decided that when the day comes for general anesthesia, we won't inform him about it. This was to prevent incidents like the one we experienced last night. We didn't want to expose the child to additional stress.

European Spartan Race Championships

Believe me, if you can boast of perseverance, you'll manage without many other advantages.

Napoleon Hill

Our life continued. One day, while writing my book, I received a message. It was an email reminder that by the end of the month, I had the last chance to register for the European Spartan Race Championships. I had completely forgotten about it. I had earned my qualification in Scotland last year, finishing 10th in my age group. It was the shortest distance of the race, measuring 5 kilometers. In practice, it usually turned out to be around 6 kilometers. The championships were scheduled to take place near London. I thought that since I was in the area, it was a great opportunity for me to participate in this race. Of course, it came at a cost.

So, I decided to sell unnecessary items to raise the money to cover the race fees. My wife was very proud of me. She was happy every time I achieved my goals in life, even the smallest ones. Coincidentally, during the competition, Eve's family was going to visit.

I was very happy. I had run Spartan Races before, but I had never had the chance to participate in the European Championships. The hardest part was telling Sebastian about it. I knew he would be unhappy and angry about it. He probably would have wanted to go as well. Unfortunately, I had no one to leave him with. Approaching my son, I knelt down beside him. I explained to him that he would get to spend time with his family during this period. But it was to no avail. He continued to walk around disappointed that he couldn't go. I promised to bring him a souvenir. He hugged me tightly and asked if I would play with his toys. Only this argument helped him understand the situation. Sebastian loved it when, each time I went on a race, I brought him something from the store. Most often, it was t-shirts with a beautiful Spartan design.

We sat on the carpet in his room. We scattered the building blocks on the floor and began to create various structures. The next day, I went for a training session. I looked at my physique. I knew that a tough race was awaiting me, and my fitness was not in its best shape. My goal was simply to finish the championships. However, what I most wanted was to see all the elite athletes in the village. The entire top field was expected to gather from different European countries. Until now, I had only seen them on social media.

I started training to prepare to the best of my ability for the competition. It was September, and I had just under a month for preparations.

I returned home tired after my training session. Natalie was playing in the living room, and Eve was resting on the couch, sipping her coffee. I took a quick shower. In a moment, I had to go pick up my son from school. I had a rushed lunch, and my wife asked me if I wanted her to brew some coffee for me. I replied that I'd like it when I got back home. I gave her a peck on the cheek and then headed to pick up Sebastian.

His day at school went very well. He didn't mention my race anymore, which surprised me a bit, as I thought he would continue to bring it up. When Sebastian finished his lunch, he asked me to go upstairs and play with his toys again.

I had the impression that after the recent incident in the hospital, Sebastian wanted me to be with him all the time when I was at home. I didn't know the reason for this. The following days passed quickly. On September 16th, the phone rang. It was Sebastian's school calling to inform us about a fundraiser they were organizing. They asked us to confirm if we had received the payment.

I logged into the portal to confirm the transfer. We thanked them for everything, for organizing the fundraiser, for being so kind and understanding when Sebastian was absent from school. I hung up, turned off the computer, and then went to the kitchen to tell Eve everything.

The preparations for the championship continued. I tried to attend training sessions regularly, but I didn't always have the time for it. Frequent visits of our children to various hospitals didn't allow me that. Yes, I could exercise at home, but it was one of the things I didn't like very much. I loved working out outside of the house. I didn't consider the home a suitable place for training.

Finally, the long-awaited day arrived for me. It was the day of departure to the European Spartan Race Championships. I checked if I had everything packed twice. I was leaving a day earlier. I had over 4 hours of driving to reach my accommodation. When I had a long distance to run, I always preferred to get a good night's sleep.

I said my goodbyes to everyone, promising to let them know once I safely arrived at my destination. About halfway through, I picked up a friend who was heading to the same place. Before reaching the hotel, I visited the sports hall in the town near the race location. There, they presented the race course and discussed obstacle rules. Many people with various flags gathered on the stage for photos. It was my first time in such a place. People had come from all over Europe for this event. At the presentation, I could already spot elite athletes. It looked entirely different from what I had seen on social media. Some were short and slim, while others were tall and more muscular. After the presentation, I picked up my race number and then went to the hotel to rest before the next day.

When I woke up in the morning, the weather wasn't favorable. It was cold, and thick fog had rolled in. I picked up my friend, who was staying at a nearby hotel, and we headed toward the village.

Once on-site, I waited for my start. My breath misted in the cold air as I did a light warm-up to avoid freezing. I was dressed in shorts and a t-shirt. Approximately halfway through the course, we had to swim across a part of the lake. I thought that if there was swimming on the course, the fewer clothes I had on, the better.

After a short warm-up, it was time to line up at the starting line. The countdown began, with loud music playing in the background.

The excitement was indescribable. I moved forward, with my sole goal being to complete the European Championships.

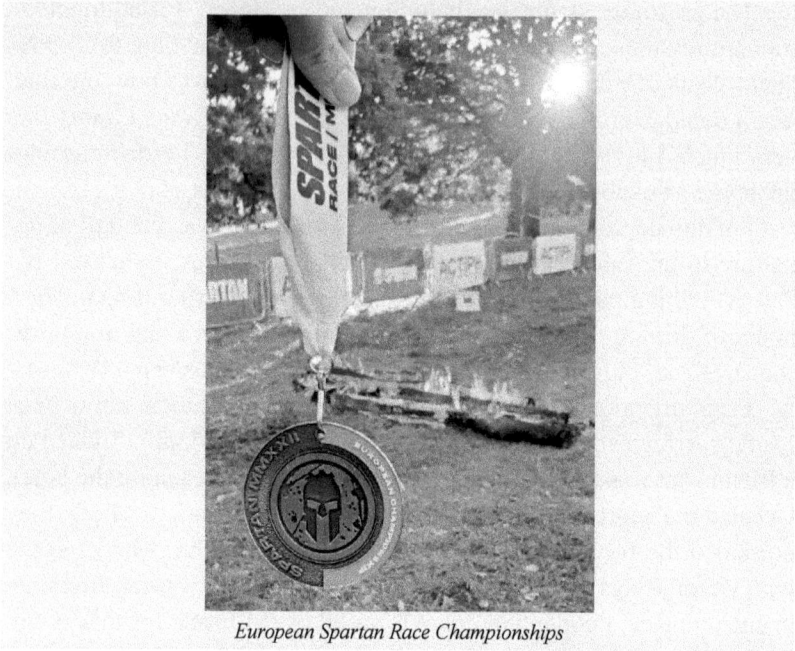

European Spartan Race Championships

As I approached the finish line, I was tired but happy. The course had taken a toll on me. Everything was going well until the swimming stage. Unfortunately, as I got out of the water and continued running, I began to experience cramps. I had to approach all the obstacles very cautiously. Time wasn't important to me, and it wasn't good. Due to the limited time I had for preparation, I didn't dwell on it.

Ahead of me was the final obstacle. I leaped over the fire and crossed the finish line. I received my long-awaited medal. As is often the case after such races, I started looking for pizza to quickly replenish my carbohydrates. However, I couldn't find any place to eat that dish. So, I quickly ordered a hot dog. I went to my car to change. It was only after I was clean that I returned to the village to look for food at my own pace and visit the souvenir shop.

I returned home around midnight. Eve and the guests were still awake. I greeted everyone, sat on the couch, and recounted my entire journey.

The End

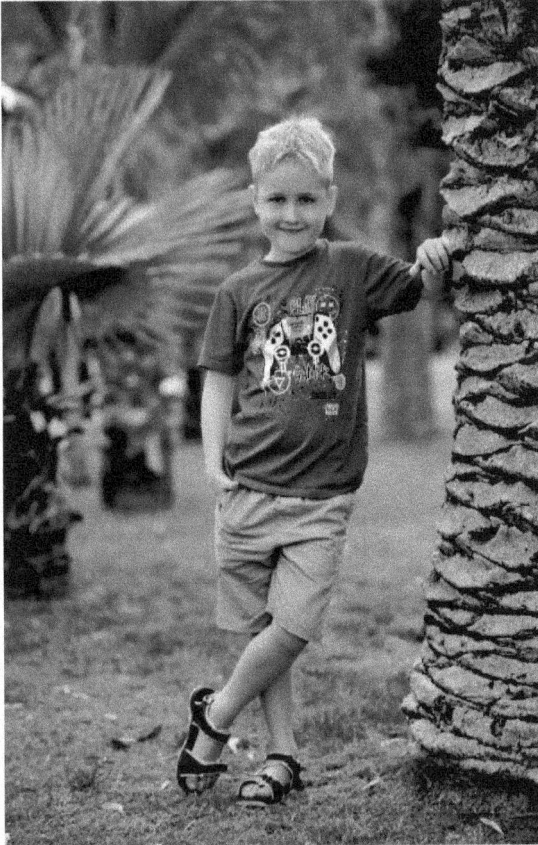

Our son, Sebastian, during the May 2023 vacation in Turkey

Appendix

*Everybody in the world is seeking happiness - and there is one
sure way to find it. That is by controlling your thoughts. Happiness
doesn't depend on outward conditions. It depends on inner
conditions.*

Dale Carnegie

Slowly, the end of the calendar year was approaching. Alongside Sebastian, sitting at the computer, we closed our last fundraiser. In total, we managed to collect over four thousand pounds! I stroked my son's hair, which had already grown back, and hugged him tightly.

Christmas was approaching. Every year, I went to a garden center to pick out a Christmas tree. They had a vast selection. I particularly cared about the shade of light green. Such a tree color perfectly matched our living room. The trunk was a bit too big, so they trimmed it for me on the spot.

Sebastian and Natalie helped with decorating the Christmas tree. They hung multicolored ornaments on the lower branches, angel figurines, and pinecones. In the end, we adorned everything with lights. Our collective effort resulted in an incredible effect. The tree was beautiful. I hugged my wife, watching our happy children playing around.

The next day, I woke up before the alarm clock. My body was slowly getting used to getting up at 5 in the morning. That's when I always brewed myself a cup of coffee and sat at the computer, writing the next chapters of my book. Even though it was Christmas Eve, I didn't plan to take a break from writing.

I spent a little over an hour at the computer, which was in my daughter's room. I didn't have a laptop, only a desktop computer.

Natalie woke up. After a moment, she sat up and smiled at me. I returned the gesture, sending her a little kiss in the process. I turned off the computer, dressed my daughter, and we went downstairs. Natalie asked me to put on her favorite cartoon. While she was watching TV, I went to the kitchen to prepare breakfast for everyone.

The day passed quickly. Eve took the children for a walk so that I could place the presents under the Christmas tree. When they returned home, they were delighted. I told them that Santa had drunk some milk, eaten a few cookies, but couldn't stay longer. In our family, it was customary for the children to open their presents only after dinner.

Outside, it was already dark. There might not have been any snow, but the holiday atmosphere was priceless.

We shared the wafer before the meal. When wishing my wife well, I thanked her for everything, for being by my side all the time, for us supporting each other. I also added that I wished for Sebastian to recover as quickly as possible and for Natalie to stand on her own two feet.

A tear rolled down my cheek. We had achieved so much this year, and there was still so much ahead of us.

We sat at the table. In the background, traditional carols were playing, and we started our meal.

For our Christmas Eve dinner, we prepared Greek-style fish, borscht with dumplings, and a slice of cake. Since we didn't have any guests this year, we didn't want to have too much food. We didn't like throwing it away. The kids didn't eat much; they were more interested in opening presents. Natalie had grown up and could eat more through her mouth, thanks to various treatments.

After dinner, we sat in the living room. Sebastian began reading the sticky notes on the presents, then distributed them to everyone.

We all sat together into the evening, watching cartoons.

A few days later, our son celebrated his 7th birthday, exactly on December 30th. He made a wish and blew out the candles. Sebastian just smiled in Natalie's direction but didn't say anything. His birthday wish remained a secret for us.

Epilogue

The most difficult thing is the decision to act, the rest is merely tenacity. The fears are paper tigers. You can do anything you decide to do. You can act to change and control your life; and the procedure, the process is its own reward.

Amelia Earhart

Natalie and her smile that never fades away

I wanted to dedicate this chapter to those who read my first book about Natalie's story. Since its conclusion, many things have changed. Natalie is now over 4 years old and doing great. What the doctors once said, that she wouldn't be able to walk on her own and would end up in a child's pushchair, can be dismissed as mere talk. Today, the little girl can walk about 300 meters while holding mine and Eve's hands. Holding onto the handles of a pushchair, she can even go 500 meters! Of course, with supervision.

Furthermore, the doctors said she wouldn't be able to feed herself. Another misconception. Our heroine has proven all the non-believers wrong. Speech specialists diagnosed that she wouldn't be able to speak clearly. Once again, the doctors in that field were mistaken. Natalie speaks very fluently. She started attending nursery school in England and quickly picked up another language.

Our life continues to move forward. There are joyful moments and there are times when we must face challenges. However, we are managing very well. I constantly strive for a better tomorrow for Natalie, so she can be as independent as possible in the future.

Sebastian (03/02/2024)

It's the possibility of having a dream come true that makes life interesting.

Paulo Coelho

Two years have passed since the diagnosis was made for my son. During this time, Sebastian has proven that despite life's adversities, one can achieve a lot.

Myself along with Sebastian

Let's start with the fact that after completing intensive treatment, he resumed running with me, and not just short distances. He preferred running 5-kilometer distances! Additionally, he began attending soccer training, a dream he had cherished for a long time. He is very interested in this sport, and my dear wife and I provided him with this opportunity. We protect the port he has under his skin with a special sponge and plaster to prevent any damage.

Sebastian is now in the 3rd grade of elementary school. Despite his long absence, he occasionally brings home diplomas for good grades. Eve and I are very proud of him. Every day, he proves that limitations exist only in our minds!

Sebastian thoroughly enjoys life, even though we have to go to the hospital for ongoing treatment from time to time. He loves traveling by train with me, collecting football cards for his album. In addition to soccer, he is passionate about fast cars. He knows almost every model and can't wait for this year's supercar festival.

Acknowledgments

Our home joys are the most delightful earth affords, and the joy of parents in their children is the most holy joy of humanity.

Johann Heinrich Pestalozzi

It wasn't easy for me to describe this whole story. Just like when I was writing my first book, emotions played the leading role. However, I managed to do it.

It's thanks to people with kind hearts that I found the strength within me to create this book.

I would like to express my immense gratitude to everyone who has been with us from the very beginning, from the moment of diagnosis, for supporting us during difficult times, for every word of encouragement you've given us.

I always read all the positive comments you write on my social media posts to the children. Thanks to you, smiles appeared on my family's faces when we were going through very challenging moments.

Sebastian's treatment is planned until mid-2025.

We keep moving forward. We don't give up. Every day, we strive for a better tomorrow.

Once again, thank you from the bottom of my heart to all of you!

I recommend

I wholeheartedly recommend my first book. You will find an incredible story of my daughter and the entire journey we had to go through in the battle for her life. This tale will deeply move you. Through reading, you will discover true love, the strength to fight, suffering, and helplessness. It is a story written straight from the heart.

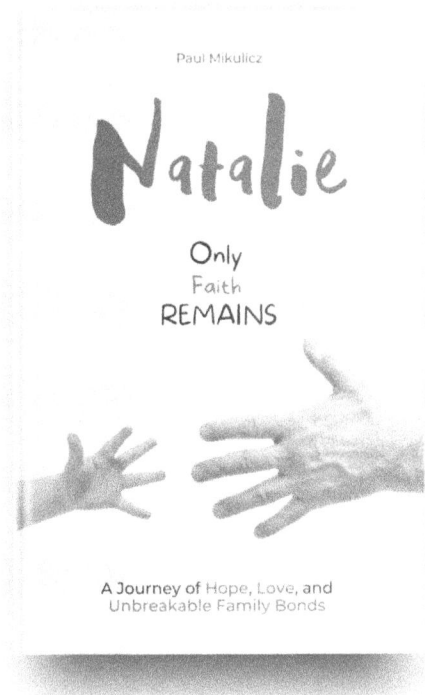

Paul Mikulicz

Natalie

Only
Faith
REMAINS

A Journey of Hope, Love, and
Unbreakable Family Bonds

All the quotes in the book are sourced from the internet.

Paul Mikulicz

The author of the book and the father of the main character is me - Paul.

In my daily life, I care for my family with all my heart. I am a sports enthusiast. My previous achievements include achieving a double trifecta in the Spartan Race in one year, completing a 5-hour Ultra Warrior run, and securing the 2nd place in an 8-kilometer trail race. My greatest sports goal is to win a medal in the Spartan Ultra Beast race. I am preparing for this event step by step.

I have plans to write more books that will help everyone who finds themselves in a similar situation.

I wish for you to keep a smile on your face that never fades away.

\

Paweł Mikulicz - Autor
pawel_mikulicz_autor

9 788397 063068